Newly Discovered Works by "William Shake-Speare," a.k.a. Edward de Vere, Earl of Oxford

by Richard M. Waugaman, M.D.

Second Edition

Text copyright © 2017 Richard M. Waugaman

**To my granddaughter,
Delphine Danielle Prieto**

ACKNOWLEDGEMENTS

I am grateful to my wife, Elisabeth Pearson Waugaman, Ph.D., for her unstinting support of my controversial Shakespeare research since 2002. Her academic background in medieval and Renaissance literature, and her brilliant capacity to think independently and creatively about literature, have been invaluable in my work.

Roger Stritmatter sparked my interest in the Shakespeare Authorship Question when his Ph.D. in Comparative Literature was the topic of an article in the *New York Times*, because his dissertation showed that Edward de Vere's Geneva Bible has annotations that are closely correlated with echoes of the Bible in Shakespeare. Roger's friendship and wise counsel have made my Shakespeare research and publications possible. Everyone who loves Shakespeare owes Roger an enormous debt of gratitude, for using academic research to shift the traditional paradigm about Shakespeare's true identity.

I am also grateful to all the fellow Oxfordians and authorship skeptics whose writings and whose encouragement have informed and inspired me. The Folger Shakespeare Library generously extended Reader's privileges to me in 2004, allowing me to do research with de Vere's Geneva Bible, and many other rare works in their unparalleled collection.

I want to thank the publications where the material in this book originally appeared: *Shakespeare Matters*; *Shakespeare Oxford Society Newsletter;* and *Brief Chronicles: An Interdisciplinary Journal of Authorship Studies.*

This second edition includes two new chapters, both attributing English translations of Latin works to de Vere (Chapters One and Three), as well as minor revisions to the rest of the book.

ABOUT THE AUTHOR

Richard M. Waugaman, M.D. is Clinical Professor of Psychiatry and 2012-2016 Faculty Expert on Shakespeare for Media Contacts at Georgetown University. He is also Adjunct Professor of Psychiatry at the Uniformed Services University of the Health Sciences; and Training and Supervising Analyst, Emeritus at the Washington Psychoanalytic Institute. He received his A.B. from Princeton, where his senior thesis on Nietzsche and Freud was supervised by Walter Kaufmann. He received his M.D. from Duke. His 170 publications include 70 articles, book chapters, and book reviews on Shakespeare and the psychology of pseudonymous authorship. Most of his Shakespeare publications are available at his websites— oxfreudian.com; and explore.georgetown.edu/people/waugamar/

TABLE OF CONTENTS

ACKNOWLEDGEMENTS

ABOUT THE AUTHOR

Chapter One

Chapter Two

A 1569 Poem, Newly Attributed to Edward de Vere

Chapter Three

Chapter Four

A Wanderlust Poem, Newly Attributed to Edward de Vere

Chapter Five

A 1578 Poem about de Vere's Trip to Italy, entitled "A Letter written by a yonge gentilwoman and sent to her husband unawares (by a freend of hers) into Italy"

Chapter Six

A Shakespearean Snail Poem, Newly Attributed to Edward de Vere

Chapter Seven

A Ribald Ignoto Poem

Chapter Eight

The Arte of English Poesie: The Case for Edward de Vere's Authorship

Chapter Nine

The Arte of Overturning Tradition: Did E.K.-- a.k.a. E.O. -- Write the Arte of English Poesie?

CONCLUSION

INTRODUCTION

When people hear that there is lively debate about who wrote the works of Shakespeare, they sometimes ask, "Oh, what difference does it make? It's the plays that really matter." Well, yes—and the poems. And the other works the same author may have written. As well as the life experiences that, blended with the author's imagination and creative genius, shaped his extraordinary works.

This book presents my research that aims to enlarge our assumptions about the canon of Shakespeare's writings. Doing so helps give us a more realistic account of the development of Shakespeare's literary career. It is unrealistic to believe, as orthodox scholars sometimes do, that everything Shakespeare wrote was of the same maturity and quality. Instead, his poetic and dramatic powers developed gradually over the course of his life.

So, I first need to review the surprisingly contentious debate about just who Shakespeare really was. Ben Jonson, that master of ambiguity, did much to confuse us, by how he introduced the first (nearly) complete collection of Shakespeare's plays, published in 1623. However, Jonson left contradictory clues, for those willing to notice them. Alexander Waugh has recently discovered that his famous phrase, "Sweet Swan of Avon," probably referred to "Avon" as the original name of Hampton Court on the Thames ("avon" is the Celtic word for "river"), where Shakespeare's plays were performed for the royal court.[1] And, when he published a folio collection of his own plays and poems in 1616, Jonson printed Shakespeare's name as "William Shake-Speare," [2]in an era when such verb-noun hyphenated names often suggested an assumed name.

We might pause to remind ourselves of the many and varied examples of books not written by their purported author. Not everyone remembers that all of the following authors used pen names: Moliere, Voltaire, Stendhal, Mark Twain, John Le Carré, George Eliot, Lewis Carroll, George Orwell, Toni Morrison, and Woody Allen. During the McCarthy era, blacklisted Hollywood screenwriters used front men as the ostensible writers of their scripts, in order to get around the ban on writing under their own names. There is also the related category of literary forgeries. The so-called Donation of Constantine was one of the most successful and long-lasting. It was an 8th century forgery by the Vatican, ostensibly a document signed by Emperor Constantine 400 years earlier, giving primacy to the Pope over the Roman Empire's secular rulers. It took this forgery some 700 years to be exposed. Then there is Thomas Rowley, the 15th century poet whose poems were actually written by the adolescent Thomas Chatterton (1752-1770), who suicided at 17 when his hoax was exposed. Castiglione's *The Book of the Courtier* was a sort of Miss Manners for the Renaissance nobility. Edward De Vere, Earl of Oxford (1550-1604)[3] sponsored a Latin translation of it, and he took the book to heart.

One central ideal for courtly behavior was *sprezzatura*, which can be translated as a façade of insouciance, or non-chalance ("sprezzare" means "to distain"). Elizabethan nobility rarely published their poems under their own names during their lifetimes. They might act in or even write court masques and interludes, and sponsor theatrical troupes for their own entertainment (and de Vere did all of the above), but they had nothing to do with *public* theaters. Openly, at least.

"There is no question whatsoever who wrote Shakespeare." "Shakespeare wrote Shakespeare!" "We know more about the life of Shakespeare than we do about the lives of most other authors of that era." "Only the lunatic fringe questions who Shakespeare was."

This is a small but representative sample of the reactions one encounters if one raises questions about who wrote Shakespeare. As a psychoanalyst with 40 years of clinical experience, I bring a psychological perspective to bear on the widespread intolerance for even asking reasonable questions about who Shakespeare was. Such a perspective is uniquely helpful in taking a step back from this bitter controversy, and looking for underlying disavowed psychodynamics.

Psychoanalysts have, with Freud, been deeply interested in Shakespeare's works. Samuel Taylor Coleridge, in fact, coined the word "psychoanalytical" to describe the richness of character in Shakespeare's works. The few psychoanalysts who have closely explored Freud's belief that Shakespeare was a pseudonym (or allonym) used by Edward de Vere (1550-1604) have indeed used a psychoanalytic approach--but in order to diagnose the "psychopathology" that led Freud into this supposedly embarrassing error.[4]

During the years since Freud's death, however, the evidence supporting his hypothesis has become impossible to ignore. For example, the discovery of de Vere's Bible resulted in a dissertation that led to the first Ph.D. in literature in the United States being awarded to a scholar who presented evidence that de Vere was Shakespeare.[5] My collaboration with him led to our recognition that there is a direct parallel between Shakespeare's interest in many obscure Biblical passages, and de Vere's interest in those same passages. That is, the more times Shakespeare quotes a given passage in the Bible, the greater the likelihood that de Vere marked that same passage in his copy of the Bible.[6] Of those Biblical passages Shakespeare echoed *once*, only 13% are marked in de Vere's Bible. But the percentage of marked verses in his Bible steadily increases as Shakespeare cites a verse more and more often—a full 88% of verses are marked for passages that Shakespeare cites *six* times.

And these are not the verses that Shakespeare's contemporaries showed special interest in. Nor was the translation read in church (the Bishop's Bible) the one that Shakespeare most often cites. True, not every Biblical passage echoed in Shakespeare is marked in de Vere's Geneva Bible. But the evidence that Shakespeare also echoed other translations strongly suggests that de Vere owned those other translations too. The psalms de Vere marked in his copy of Sternhold and Hopkins' *Whole Booke of the Psalms* (WBP) correlate highly with previously unnoticed allusions to those psalms in the Sonnets, plays, and *The Rape of Lucrece*.[7] This psalter was metrical, and included the music to which they were sung. It was extremely popular in the Elizabethan era. It was bound with many Bibles, including de Vere's. De Vere marked 14 psalms with ornate, distinctive "manicules," or pointing hands.[8]

Among my findings about these psalm echoes are that Psalm 137 is echoed several times in *Richard II*;[9] *Titus Andronicus* repeatedly echoes Psalm 6; Lady Macbeth's "Out damned spot" speech echoes Psalm 51 (the "chief penitential psalm"); Sonnet 21 is structured as a response to Psalm 8 (so, in this case, the psalmist is "that Muse," who was previously assumed to be some contemporary rival poet); in *Henry VI, Part One*, Joan of Arc echoes psalms not only in the beginning of the play, when she is saintly, but even when she is invoking demons in Act V.

Orthodox reactions to an ultimately successful challenge of a cherished paradigm often pass through three stages, namely: (1) "That's absurd!"; (2) "What difference would it make??"; and finally, (3) "Of course-- I always said that!" We do not assume that saying "Mark Twain wrote Mark Twain" eliminates the role of Samuel Clemens in those works. No one has found a single piece of evidence from Shakespeare's lifetime that proves conclusively that anyone thought he was a writer.[10] Contemporary references to "Shakespeare" were in all likelihood references to the pseudonym that began appearing in 1593. What we know about the traditional Shakspere of Stratford from the historical record shows no connections with a literary career. The long history of ad hominem attacks on anyone who challenges traditional beliefs about who wrote Shakespeare have grown more vicious, more frequent, and more desperate as the traditional authorship theory has been collapsing. Once we become better acquainted with the weakness of orthodox evidence, this shameful bullying becomes more understandable.

Literary studies lack a methodology that offers definitive reliability and validity in assessing evidence for authorship. Further, scholars who have staked their careers and reputations on traditional authorship beliefs are bound to encounter severe cognitive dissonance when they try to weigh contrary evidence objectively. As a result, power, authority, "groupthink"[11], and personal influence all play prominent roles in public positions on authorship on the part of Shakespeare scholars who have academic careers. Winning a Ph.D. in English; being hired, published, promoted, and respected by one's peers may all be jeopardized by expressing "heretical" opinions on authorship. One English teacher confided in me that it would be "professional suicide" for a graduate student in English to admit to being an authorship doubter. Ironically, John Keats famously said, in a letter to his brothers George and Thomas on December 22, 1817, "Shakespeare possessed so enormously... *Negative Capability*, that is when man is capable of being in uncertainties, Mysteries, doubts, without any irritable reaching after fact & reason."[12] Yet most scholars show little capacity to tolerate doubt as to authorship.

Genuine openness to the evidence requires a willingness to question one's assumptions. Orthodox Shakespeareans, however, unwittingly demonstrate a fixation in a medieval form of reasoning from the unquestionable premise of accepting the traditional author. Consequently, they continue to follow the sort of Aristotelian *de*ductive reasoning that begins with an unquestioned premise. They do not put into practice the newer Renaissance methodology of *in*ductive reasoning based on an objective assessment of all the evidence. None of us is immune to blind spots for the powerful way our assumptions skew our perceptions of evidence.

Since the Enlightenment, we typically turn to the scientific method as the gold standard for an objective assessment of the evidence in any field. We assume science, when compared to literary studies, possesses a more reliable methodology for evaluating new theories. Ironically, scientists, being human, often fall short of this ideal themselves. The history of virtually any topic in science shows a disturbing pattern of scientists ignoring, explaining away, or suppressing new evidence that contradicts a prevailing theory. As a result of the groupthink of scientists, it is sometimes an outsider who is open to discovering a new paradigm that is later validated. The editor of *Science News* wrote, "Scientists sometimes cringe at revelations of their fallibility. But it's how science works, and how it works best. Science's great strength is the willingness to submit [observations to further] scrutiny. Nonscientists in any number of other fields might want to ponder whether the world would be better off if they had the same attitude." [13]

Recall that Alfred Wegener had accumulated overwhelming evidence for his theory of continental drift by 1915. He was a mere geographer, though, not a geologist. Geologists, the specialists in that field, argued that there was no known conceivable explanation of how continental drift could have occurred, so they ridiculed Wegener's theory. But, by the mid-1960's, new information about plate tectonics provided the missing pieces of explanatory theory, and geologists now fully accept Wegener's brilliant and well documented 1915 proposal. Every field of science has similar cautionary stories about the initial rejection of new, valid ideas. As another example, Lord Kelvin was considered such a brilliant scientist that his calculation that the earth was less than 100 million years old threatened to invalidate Charles Darwin's theory of evolution through natural selection.

The situation is analogous when it comes to de Vere as "Shake-Speare." We have good evidence that he was regarded by his contemporaries as one of the best Elizabethan courtier poets; that a few of his contemporaries knew he wrote anonymously; that he sponsored theatrical companies most of his life, as did his father and grandfather; and that he was regarded as one of the best Elizabethan authors of comedies. There are hundreds of connections between the content of the plays and poems of Shakespeare and the documented facts of de Vere's life. *But*, we still do not know with certainty why he wrote under a pen name. This crucial but missing piece of evidence is a major reason that de Vere is not yet more widely accepted as Shakespeare.

In all likelihood, there were multiple internal and external reasons for de Vere using a pseudonym. According to Marcy North's important research,[14] most books published in 16th century England did not include the author's name. They were published anonymously, or with a pseudonym. Among the possible reasons for this tradition was the controversial nature of a book. Many authors in the era, including Ben Jonson, were punished for offending those in power. Most Elizabethan nobility did not publish poetry under their names during their lifetimes. The world of the theater was held in some disrepute. De Vere/Shakespeare's history plays put the Tudor monarchs in the best possible light; their propaganda value may have been enhanced by attributing them to a commoner. In addition, the study of the psychology of pseudonymity offers many examples of writers whose creativity seemed to flourish when their authorship was concealed. If de Vere used one pseudonym, he probably disguised other writings as well. In this book, I attribute several anonymous 16th-century poems to de Vere/Shakespeare, as well as *The Arte of English Poesie*. In addition, I have suggested that the two "Ignoto" poems ("The First" and "The Burning") and the immediately following Shakespeare poem "Let the bird of loudest lay" in *Love's Martyr* were all written by de Vere.[15]

David Ellis, Emeritus Professor of English at the University of Kent at Canterbury, closely examines the lack of evidence underlying recent Shakespeare biographies by Peter Ackroyd, Jonathan Bate, Katherine Duncan-Jones, Stephen Greenblatt, James Shapiro, and René Weis.[16] Ellis whimsically points to "the trend whereby biography [of Shakespeare] becomes a prize for those Shakespeareans from the Academy who had become eminent in their profession. Given the limitations of data with which they then had to deal, this was if highly trained athletes were required to qualify at [an] international level so that they could then participate in an annual British sack race."[17] Ellis is critical of these Shakespeare biographers who capitalize on the public hunger to find out more about Shakespeare than we actually know. In the process, he charges, there is "a general lowering of intellectual standards and the degradation of the art of biography."[18] These are serious charges.

Bruce Danner is another mainstream Shakespeare scholar who refutes his traditional biography. In his chapter, "The Anonymous Shakespeare: Heresy, Authorship, and the Anxiety of Orthodoxy," he provocatively claims anonymity for the plays attributed to Shakespeare because he views "the construction of Shakespeare as a vague, colossal abstraction so capacious as to become undefineable."[19] Danner adds that "the Shakespearean profession itself is the author of anti-Stratfordianism. In its vision of Shakespeare as author, professional scholars can neither portray nor theorize the figure beyond the sphere of anonymity."[20] One of Danner's first lines of attack is against the foundation stone of orthodoxy, the 1623 First Folio. Without it, the orthodox case collapses. Danner admits that "the First Folio falsifies a number of key facts" ;[21] its "omissions, errors, and outright lies have long been common knowledge."[22] He singles out Stephen Greenblatt for scathing criticism of Greenblatt's specious and contradictory discussion of other literary evidence. He says Greenblatt "ventures into novel avenues of myth-making that undermine his position in creative new ways"[23] and that "Greenblatt's views look less like theories than desperate overreaching."[24] Danner charges that Stratfordians have not established the chronology of the plays; they are ignorant as to the author's political, religious, and cultural opinions; and that they cannot establish the authorial text for the plays. "Such facts provide the foundations of literary study... and yet these are just such definitive issues that the Shakespearean profession cannot resolve."[25]

Despite his deserved eminence as a Shakespeare scholar, Greenblatt writes misleadingly that the dedications of the long poems (*Venus and Adonis* and *The Rape of Lucrece*) "are the only such documents from Shakespeare's hand."[26] A trusting reader might falsely assume Greenblatt means "in Shakespeare's handwriting." There has been no new evidence linking "Hand D" in one manuscript page of the play *Sir Thomas More* with Shakespeare. Nevertheless, the Royal Shakespeare Company 2007 edition of the complete plays of Shakespeare now makes the unsupported claim that this page *is* in Shakespeare's handwriting (not that it "might be"). The claim is speculative, because the only samples we have that may *possibly* be in his handwriting are six signatures-- but even the highly respected Shakespeare scholar Samuel Schoenbaum eventually admitted that each signature is different, and each even used different spelling. So it cannot be known with certainty that *any* of these signatures is genuine, much less that Hand D is in Shakespeare's handwriting. (In fact, some of its spelling idiosyncrasies are consistent with those of de Vere's letters. De Vere's spelling was eccentric, even by Elizabethan norms; it is thus one source of evidence in evaluating authorship.)

What follows is a brief, highly selective overview of the history of assumptions as to the authorship of Shakespeare's works. This history is not well known, but it is essential in understanding the psychology of "orthodox" reactions when their tenuous authorship beliefs are questioned. I will highlight those aspects of this history that are most problematic in confusing our search for the actual author of the works.

Since many critics consider the Sonnets to be the most autobiographical of Shakespeare's works, it is instructive to ponder their fate.[27] Only 13 copies of the first 1609 edition survive. The Sonnets did not appear again until 1640, when John Benson published a tellingly mutilated version of them. Most significantly, he tried to transform most of the 126 homosexual love poems into heterosexual love poems. Eight of these he omitted completely, including a current favorite ("Shall I compare thee to a summer's day?"). It is often argued rather unpersuasively that only friendship is meant in the first 126 Sonnets. If so, Benson would not have needed to redact the Sonnets as he did. Benson, in 1640, surely knew more about how the original versions of these poems would be interpreted by his contemporaries than do today's scholars who claim they have no biographically relevant bisexual content. It was only in 1780 that Malone restored the Sonnets to their original wording; he stated explicitly that 120 of them [sic] were addressed to a man.

There are few indications of any serious, widespread interest in knowing who wrote Shakespeare's works during his lifetime, or during the next century.[28] The first brief biographical sketches were written in the early 18th century, starting with that by John Aubrey, then by Nicholas Rowe. But a century had passed, so there were few reliable eye-witness accounts available to biographers. What they recorded instead were "legends" about Shakespeare, that were often accepted into the biographical record, with little evidence to attest to their veracity. Most significantly, no one ever thought it necessary to present evidence that the plays and poems were in fact written by the traditional author. This never proven assumption continues up to the present day, creating massive circularity.[29] For example, it is assumed that Shakespeare from Stratford was the author, therefore it is assumed (without any real evidence) that he *must* have attended the Stratford grammar school (but literacy was an entrance requirement, and his parents were illiterate).

The first major turning point in popular interest in Shakespeare was in 1769. It is helpful to recall the context of that period in English intellectual history. By then, the Enlightenment had dealt a mortal blow to intellectuals' traditional religious beliefs, leaving something of a void. Enter David Garrick, the most prominent Shakespeare actor of the 18th century. He fostered a cult of personality, skillfully linking himself with Shakespeare the man, raising the public profile of both Shakespeare and Garrick. He commissioned paintings, medallions, and etchings that placed his likeness with Shakespeare's. Garrick brought the apotheosis of Shakespeare to a climax by holding the first Stratford "Jubilee" in 1769. This event succeeded in putting Stratford on the map as a sort of secular pilgrimage site (and ever since, with its 4 million annual tourists, its vast economic self-interest in maintaining the traditional authorship theory cannot be ignored).

Garrick was equally successful in enlarging and perpetuating the assumption that Shakspere of Stratford was the author of Shakespeare's works. Prior to 1769, Shakespeare was associated primarily with London, rather than with Stratford. The new fascination with Shakespeare's alleged birthplace captured the emerging interest in Shakespeare the person. Previously, popular sentiment seemed to be an earlier version of the current, dismissive "What difference would it make who wrote the works of Shakespeare?"

During the following century in Britain, biography in general became popular for the first time. Further, the potentially disruptive effect of increased literacy in the lower social classes was probably attenuated by a widely shared belief that Britain's greatest writer was a commoner. In the United States, a dark tradition of anti-intellectualism seems still to undergird the angry reluctance to question who Shakespeare was.

In 1597, Thomas Deloney published *Jack of Newbury*, a book that paved the way for the acceptance of the traditional Shakespeare authorship myth following the 1623 publication of Shakespeare's First Folio. Deloney's book was extremely popular, going through some sixteen editions by 1700. It told the appealing, rags to riches story of a 16th century Horatio Alger figure, John Winchcomb of Newbury (1489-1557), who in reality began as a simple workman and rose to great heights of wealth and renown. He built England's first factory; turned down a knighthood offered by King Henry VIII; and became one of England's wealthiest and most influential cloth merchants. The popularity of Deloney's fictionalized account of Winchcomb's life probably enhanced the related appeal of the legend that the Merchant of Stratford became the nation's greatest writer.

I do not exaggerate when I refer to the "apotheosis" of Shakespeare. As Christian Deelman writes, "The importance of the [1769] Jubilee in the history of Shakespeare's reputation can hardly be exaggerated. It marks the point at which Shakespeare stopped being regarded as an increasingly popular and admirable dramatist, *and became a god.*"[30]

I believe this is one of the most crucial dimensions of the psychology of traditional belief in Shakespeare. George Romney's 1789 painting, "The Infant Shakespeare, Surrounded by Nature and the Passions" powerfully illustrates this phenomenon.[31] It was painted twenty years after Garrick's Stratford Jubilee. It is obviously modeled on nativity scenes of Jesus, with the infant Shakespeare taking the place of the baby Jesus. It was surely not because of its aesthetic merits that Henry Folger paid six times more for this painting than for any other work of art in his collection (the largest collection of Shakespearean art in the world). He undoubtedly sensed a much more psychological or spiritual, rather than artistic appeal in this painting. (Yet Folger was open-minded enough to purchase de Vere's Bible when it was offered to him.)

What does this apotheosis of Shakespeare have to do with the issue of authorship? Everything. It conveys a subtle implication that Shakespeare's works are like the Bible, making Shakespeare a sort of secular deity. We often speak of "the Bible and Shakespeare" in one breath as the greatest works of our literature. We are usually unaware, though, that we treat Shakespeare's works as *equivalent* to the Bible in many ways. They are a secular Bible, for anyone skeptical about the theological status of our traditional Bible. The thousands of biblical echoes in the words, phrases, and ideas in Shakespeare's works deepen this link. Who wrote the Bible? Traditionally, God inspired it. Human beings wrote it down, but believers maintain that God is its true author.

If God wrote the Bible, it is largely irrelevant which human beings took His dictation. Similarly, Shakspere of Stratford serves so perfectly in the role of author of Shakespeare's works because he had to be divinely inspired, given his lack of formal education and exposure to the court; noble hobbies such as hawking; travel to Italy; etc. that are clearly evident in the canon. Romney's "nativity" painting of Shakespeare embodies 18th century belief that Shakespeare proved that genius stems from Nature, not from Nurture.

An important precursor of this misunderstanding goes all the way back to ancient Greece. In Plato's dialogue *The Apology*, Socrates claims that poets and reciters of poetry show no grasp of the significance of their poems. Socrates deduces that poets must therefore be divinely inspired, contributing little from their own minds (or life experiences) to their poetry. According to Plato, Socrates said, "I decided it was not wisdom that enabled them to write their poetry, but a kind of instinct or inspiration, such as you find in seers and prophets."[32] In the dialogue *Ion*, Socrates cites a poet who wrote only one good poem, and he concludes that this proves "the god would show us... that these lovely poems are not of man or human workmanship, but are divine and from the gods, and that the poets are nothing but interpreters of the gods... to prove this, the deity on purpose sang the loveliest of all lyrics through the most miserable poet."[33]

When thoughtful people became alarmed by finding no facts about Shakspere's life that had any connection with his literary works, they were told they simply did not understand the nature of artistic genius. A real genius, they were informed, uses his imagination, not irrelevant life experiences. He is inspired by his creative imagination. Traditional religious belief, including in the Bible as the inspired Word of God, unconsciously paved the way for acceptance of Shakespeare as an implicitly secular, surrogate deity. The loss of traditional religious beliefs helped to enthrone Shakspere as "Shakespeare." And "heretics" are still persecuted by those in power.

After 1769, as I said, there was an increasingly desperate thirst to learn more about the "divine" Shakespeare. When each well that was dug proved to be dry, along came William Henry Ireland. In 1795, he showed to scholars a treasure trove of Shakespeare letters and other documents, proving beyond doubt that Shakespeare wrote Shakespeare. James Boswell was so moved that he kneeled before the documents. The Poet Laureate and other luminaries signed a "Certificate of *Belief*" (emphasis added) attesting to the authenticity of these documents. They must have felt crushed when Ireland admitted a year later that he had forged everything.

In 1831, John Payne Collier said of Shakespeare, "the first observation that must be made is, that so few facts are extant regarding him."[34] Collier soon rectified this embarrassing lack of facts. In 1835, he published his electrifying discovery of previously unknown primary documents concerning Shakespeare. During the ensuing 20 years, he continued finding more and more documents that provided precisely the previously missing information about Shakespeare as a *literary* person. Collier's discoveries catapulted his reputation to the highest echelon of Shakespeare scholars.

Just when Shakspere's status as Shakespeare was finally being established securely, the claim of the man from Stratford suddenly and nearly disastrously collapsed. Collier, like W.H. Ireland, was found to have *forged* all the documents he claimed to have discovered. In retrospect, one can hardly blame him or Ireland. Although ambitious and dishonest, they were also filling a deep need in admirers of Shakespeare to have some relics they could revere, while never doubting their faith that they had the right author.

All these forgeries seem in fact to have gained an undeserved form of immortality, in *still* contributing to the widespread but mistaken belief that we have unquestioned documentation of who Shakespeare was. Like the century in which all editions of the Sonnets made them love poems to a woman, "evidence" that has since been discredited lives on, since it meets such powerful psychological needs as to who we *want* Shakespeare to be. The Stratfordian Jack Lynch states that "Some of the misinformation [Collier] introduced into his works in the 1830s continues to circulate in books and articles today. Lies, once they are accepted as true, take on a life of their own, one that lasts long after the original falsehoods have been exposed... It's reasonable to assume that many of the 'facts' about Shakespeare and his age were not discovered but invented... It should give us pause any time we think our knowledge about Shakespeare is on firm ground." Lynch stops short of reaching the conclusion I am advocating: that Shakespeare was not in fact the man from Stratford.[35]

In 1857, as Collier's forgeries were unraveling, Delia Bacon published the first book to challenge Shakspere of Stratford as the author Shakespeare. Disillusionment over Ireland's and then Collier's false claims threatened to undermine traditional beliefs about authorship, repeating the loss of belief in God a century earlier. I suspect it made many open-minded intellectuals receptive to the first serious challenges to "orthodox" assumptions. Some of the most prominent authors of the 19th century became persuaded that, whoever he was, Shakespeare the author was *not* the man from Stratford. The list includes Walt Whitman, Henry James, and Mark Twain. Nathaniel Hawthorne wrote a preface to Bacon's 1857 book and helped get it published. Challenges to orthodox authorship beliefs have only increased since Bacon's book. Although Francis Bacon has not been accepted as Shakespeare, a new era in authorship scholarship blossomed. It was about 60 years later before someone first proposed Edward de Vere, Earl of Oxford, as Shakespeare, and his claim is increasingly accepted. The more that is learned about de Vere, the more convincing his authorship claim has become.

One of the 19th century's foremost Shakespeare scholars was Sidney Lee. In his 1898 biography of Shakespeare, he discussed the forgeries by Collier and his predecessors-- "The intense interest which Shakespeare's life and work have long universally excited has tempted unprincipled or sportively mischievous writers from time to time to deceive the public by the forgery of documents purporting to supply new information. The forgers were especially active at the end of the [18th] century and during the middle years of the [19th] century."[36]

Note the phrase "sportively mischievous." Lee is too forgiving of Ireland and Collier. Then, immediately after his summary of the Shakespeare forgeries, Lee turns to the authorship controversy. Lee helped begin the lively and continuing tradition of *ad hominem* in lieu of substantive, *ad rem* counterarguments. He was writing at a time when he had to argue against Bacon as the only other alleged author of Shakespeare's works. But the tone of Lee's arguments set the precedent that has been followed ever since in attacking subsequent "heresies." His four pages on the topic begin by referring to the "fantastic theory" that Shakespeare's works were not written by Shakespeare. He calls such a theory "perverse." He also calls theories that question traditional authorship "strange," "unintelligible," "arbitrary and baseless," and argues that they have "no rational right to a hearing." He speaks of "the only sane interpretation" of a letter to Francis Bacon, that contradicts his claim to be Shakespeare. Lee continues in the next paragraph, "Miss Delia Bacon, who was the first to spread abroad a spirit of skepticism respecting the established facts [sic] of Shakespeare's career, died insane."[37] Notice the insinuation that heretics who dare question the "facts" may be insane. I would suggest that Lee's invective stems from the defensiveness of orthodox Shakespeare scholars, when having been taken in by Ireland's and Collier's forgeries for decades weakened their credibility, and planted seeds of doubt among the general public. The rage of Shakespeare scholars toward the forgers, I would suggest, continues to be redirected onto authorship skeptics.

Lee was one of the first Shakespeare scholars to argue we should dissociate the author's life experiences from his literary works. Given a complete lack of fit between the traditional author's life and the works, Lee suggested we should not expect to find any such correspondence-- "it is dangerous to read into Shakespeare's dramatic utterances allusions to his personal experience."... "to assume that he wrote...from practical experience... is to underrate his intuitive power of realising life under almost every aspect *by force of his imagination*"[38] (Lee's emphasis). Lee noted the striking financial success of the man from Stratford. That fact has at least indirectly contributed to the assumption that he was the author—Max Weber famously observed that we often regard financial success as a sign that one was divinely favored.[39]

Augustus Ralli summarizes Lee's thesis that Shakespeare did not write from personal experience: "There is no tangible evidence that Shakespeare's tragic period [of plays] had a personal cause... The external facts of his life show unbroken progress of prosperity... To seek in *mere personal experience* the key to his conquest of the topmost peaks of tragedy is to underrate his creative faculty and disparage the force of its magic [sic]... Shakespeare's dramatic work is impersonal, and does not show his idiosyncrasies... [There is] no self-evident revelation of personal experiences of emotion or passion [my emphasis]."[40]

Ralli tentatively voices his reservations about Lee's categorical rejection of Shakespeare's personal experiences as influencing his creative works-- "[Lee] has been beguiled by his own phrases... it seems to us that he pondered the subject till his subconscious mind gathered force and supplied the best words for one solution, so that he became self-convinced and slightly overstated what after all belongs to conjecture." One of the most puzzling aspects of Lee's position is that it represented a complete reversal from his earlier opinions, at least concerning the Sonnets. Initially, Lee held that "In [all but two of] the Sonnets Shakespeare avows... the experiences of his own heart." A few months later, Lee now said the Sonnets only created "the illusion of personal confession." I would speculate that homophobia played a role in Lee's reversal-- to read the Sonnets as autobiography confronts the objective reader with unavoidable evidence of the poet's bisexuality. Interestingly, Lee himself may have been gay, but in the closet.

An anonymous author wrote in 1909, in reviewing a book that challenged the traditional authorship assumption,

"Let us frankly admit that there are puzzles in regard to Shakespeare's classical attainments, his knowledge of travel, and his knowledge of law. The biographers of Shakespeare without a doubt have been at fault here. Let us suppose for the sake of argument that there are one thousand ascertainable facts about Shakespeare. Of these Rowe, in 1709, discovered ten, of which seven have since been found to be more or less erroneous. The biographers of today are in possession, let us say, of about forty, and on the strength of these and their own ingenuity they presume to answer every conceivable puzzle that confronts the observer of the dramatist's career.... It makes us forget those very simple words that ought so often to be on our lips, '*We don't know.*' The ingenuity of the biographers is pleasing and even plausible, but its projections are like the Shakespeare portraits-- no two are alike and the latest word of the last expert is that they are all fabrications, not to say impostures [reviewer's emphasis]."[41]

The role of "legend" is Shakespeare biographies is fascinating. Most strikingly, the foremost 20th century Shakespeare biographer, Samuel Schoenbaum, was dismissive of anyone who introduced what he considered to be excessive speculation in their studies of Shakespeare's life. "[My] book... differs from most of the innumerable popular biographies of Shakespeare that *augment the facts with speculation* [my emphasis]."[42] It is surely no coincidence that new, highly speculative biographies of Shakespeare have proliferated since Schoenbaum's death in 1996.

Nevertheless, Schoenbaum justified *his* inclusion of legends in Shakespeare's story-- "Much of this [legendary and apocryphal] material is quite simply good fun, but the workings of myth have a place in the historical record, and may sometimes conceal elusive germs of truth."[43] He actually once used the phrase "was indeed probably,"[44] a testament to his struggle to extract definite facts from what was unproven. Schoenbaum divided legends into plausible and implausible categories. He made this judgment based on his circular assumption that Shakespeare the author was Shakspere of Stratford.

In the process, he rejected a wonderful story that gains in plausibility if one exercises skepticism as to the traditional theory of authorship. During a performance before Queen Elizabeth, the Queen was so determined to get "Shakespeare's" attention that she walked up to him on stage, dropped her glove, and blocked his path. "Shakespeare" picked up her glove and returned it to her, while improvising two lines of iambic pentameter-- "And though now bent on this high embassy,/ Yet *stoop* we to take up our Cousin's glove!"[45] Schoenbaum argues against the veracity of this legend by claiming that "the Queen is not known to have professed admiration for Shakespeare ... and she restrained herself publicly (as in private) from flirtations with subjects of inferior station."[46] Alternatively, we can hypothesize the story *is* accurate, then reach a different conclusion about the playwright and actor's social class. If these are words that de Vere actually improvised, they give us an astonishing example of his skill at verbal improvisation, comparable to Bach's legendary genius for improvising on the organ. The words contain multiple puns. We might notice that the Queen referred to de Vere as "Our said *Cousin*" in her June 26, 1586 document granting him his pension of £1,000 per year.

I assume that the name "Shakespeare" also alluded to de Vere's acting, at least at court. No one has found any documentary evidence that Shakespeare acted after 1603, which is consistent with de Vere's death in 1604. The 1825 record which Schoenbaum quotes for his anecdote stated, "It is well known that Queen Elizabeth was a great admirer of the immortal Shakspeare."[47] The historical record leaves no doubt that she was in fact a great admirer of de Vere-- they may have had an affair, for which Elizabeth was rebuked in a letter from her sister. The Queen loved the perfumed gloves de Vere gave her when he returned from Italy-- "She took such pleasure in these gloves that she was pictured with them upon her hands, and for many years afterwards it was called the 'Earl of Oxford's perfume'."[48] Ben Jonson's collected works of 1616 list "William Shake-Speare" as one of the principal actors in *Sejanus*. Since that play allegedly had a co-author who was never named, de Vere may have been that co-author, and listing "Shake-Speare" as an actor in it may have been Jonson's veiled way of giving credit to de Vere.

Schoenbaum was merciless in his ad hominem denigration of anyone who questions the traditional author. One of his milder attacks was on the "pattern of psychopathology" with "paranoid structures of thought" that he discovered in "recurring features of anti-Stratfordian behavior."[49] He also invoked the language of religious dogma in calling authorship skeptics "heretics" and "schismatics." Is he protesting a bit too much?

Where do things stand now in the world of orthodox Stratfordians? Paul Edmondson and Stanley Wells of the Shakespeare Birthplace Trust have recently edited a book that brazenly claims there is no doubt whatsoever about the traditional authorship theory. In their fury against authorship doubters, they call them "anti-Shakespearean," deliberately insinuating that skeptics are against not only their authorship theory, but the author himself. They seem unaware of an April 22, 2007 *New York Times* survey of 265 United States Shakespeare professors, that found only 82% of them *when responding anonymously* said "there is no good reason to question" the Stratfordian theory.[50] Such are the intellectually questionable tactics used to shore up the traditional authorship theory.

So, what difference does it make who wrote the works of Shakespeare? A world of difference. Shakespeare scholarship has been marred by a series of blind spots. One can trace these blind spots over the centuries of Shakespeare criticism. The myth that nature alone, not education, produced his genius has led to a systematic devaluation of the extent of his scholarship and of the many books in several languages that influenced his works. Lee spoke for many Shakespeare scholars in discouraging us from looking for any links between the literary works and the author's life experiences. The Sonnets, especially, have elicited impassioned denials of any autobiographical connections.   Respected literary scholars have *denied* that there is any connection between the plays and contemporary political events; that the author needed to have travelled abroad to know first-hand the many places in Italy he wrote about;[51] that he needed any special knowledge of law;[52] that the Bible influenced his works; that he could read Italian or ancient Greek; or that he could have read widely at all. Essentially, a "dumbing down" of Shakespeare.

But all these assumptions have been shown to be false. Stuart Gillespie has published a 500-page supplement to past scholarship on Shakespeare's literary sources.[53] Scholars can no longer deny Shakespeare's truly phenomenal erudition. It is now accepted that he read several foreign languages, and engaged in astonishingly nuanced debates on scholarly controversies in theology, literary theory, medicine, history, astronomy, and other subjects. In his Geneva Bible, de Vere crossed out one word and substituted the translation of the Latin Vulgate Bible. His eminent childhood tutors were amazed by his intellect. The depth and complexity of his plays increases exponentially when we can link them with the author's life.

Sadly, the need to ignore the person who wrote the works has lessened scholarly interest in Shakespeare's poetry, which was more popular during his lifetime than were his plays. His long poems outsold the early editions of his plays. The pseudonym "Shakespeare" appeared in print for the first time as the author of "Venus and Adonis," in 1593. Stritmatter has persuasively argued that this poem is a thinly disguised account of de Vere's affair with Queen Elizabeth.[54] It is understandable that he did not publish it under his own name.

I have offered a sample of the systematic distortions that unquestioned traditional authorship assumptions have introduced into our understanding of Shakespeare and his works. It may be "painful," as Freud experienced, to relinquish the comfort of our long-held assumptions about who Shakespeare was. But tolerating the disruptions of this paradigm shift is well worth it. There will be a renaissance in Shakespeare studies as we deal with the authorship question more objectively. Everyone who loves Shakespeare, and loves the pursuit of the truth, should welcome this renaissance.

Finally, a word of practical advice—if you are new to Kindle and e-readers, the endnotes are readily accessible by simply touching their respective numbers; you can easily return to your place in the book.

Chapter One

Edward de Vere Translated Ovid's *Metamorphoses*: Hendiadys and Other Philological Evidence

Hendiadys is "*not* a very common figure in Ovid" (Owen, 83; emphasis added).[55] But it abounds in the English translation of Ovid's *Metamorphoses* signed by Arthur Golding, which many of us attribute to the young de Vere, Golding's nephew.[56] In it (including its Preface), de Vere introduces 390 word pairs that are not found earlier in EEBO.[57] "Hendiadys" refers to a particular sort of word pair, defined by the OED as "a figure of speech in which a single complex idea is expressed by two words connected by a conjunction." The first two uses of the word "hendiadys" given by the OED are in the 1589 *Arte of English Poesie*,[58] which I have attributed to de Vere;[59] and the 1592 *The English Secretary* by Angel Day, who was de Vere's literary secretary.[60] Hendiadys is found more often in Shakespeare than in any other Elizabethan writer, so its profusion in the "Golding" Ovid is presumptive evidence of de Vere's authorship of this noted translation.

Books One through Four of that translation appeared in 1565, when de Vere was only fifteen. Its dedicatory epistle states that it was written at Cecil House, when both de Vere and his maternal uncle Arthur Golding lived there.

John F. Nims, in his Introduction to the "Golding" *Metamorphoses*,[61] muses about the flagrant paradox of Golding, the "convinced Puritan who spent much of his life translating the sermons and commentaries of John Calvin" undertaking to English this work of Ovid, "the sophisticated darling of a dissolute society, the author of a scandalous handbook of seduction [i.e., *The Art of Love*] (xiv). Unwittingly assisting the re-attribution of this translation to Golding's precocious nephew, Nims calls this notion "Hardly less striking than the metamorphoses the work dealt with" (xiv), especially given how much racier this translation is than Ovid's original. Similarly, Raphael Lyne concludes that, in contrast with the usual tradition of *Ovid moralisé*, "Golding [sic] almost invariably does not insinuate moral interpetations into Ovid's stories" (29).[62] Surprising indeed, if the Puritan was the actual translator. Lyne also makes the intriguing observation that the translator—unlike Ovid—tried to indicate dialect pronunciation at certain points. E.g., "a swap of 'z' for 's'" (57) in Book XV, 750-756. *King Lear* uses this same substitution, to indicate a Somersetshire dialect. I strongly doubt that Arthur Golding had this sort of ear for dialect pronunciation, or made use of it in any of his other works. But Shake-speare did. .

Unfortunately, our attribution of many Elizabethan works became set in concrete before more recent scholarship on anonymous, pseudonymous, and allonymous Elizabethan authorship was more fully appreciated.[63] No doubt, some of his contemporaries knew de Vere was the real translator, and that was probably one reason that Shake-speare was known to his contemporaries as an "English Ovid"[64] (Ogburn, 1984, 443).

We might pause a moment to ask if it is conceivable that a boy of fifteen could possibly have composed the first four books of this translation. Yes, since we are talking about the greatest writer in the history of English literature. Studies of the psychology of creativity have concluded that childhood loss often contributes to creativity in talented individuals. De Vere lost his father three years before his translation of Ovid first appeared. And turning to a work written 1,500 years earlier may have offered de Vere something of an escape from the many stresses in his young life.

In any event, there have been child prodigies in many creative fields, including literature. One thinks of the English poet Thomas Chatterton (1752-1770), who took his own life at seventeen after his forgeries of the poems of an invented medieval monk were exposed. Or the French poet, Arthur Rimbaud (1854-1891). One of his best poems ("Ophélie") was composed when he was only fifteen, and he finished his creative writing by the age of twenty. A third example is Mary Shelly, who wrote her classic *Frankenstein* when she was only nineteen. Elisabeth Sears[65] has even proposed that the ten-year-old de Vere wrote the 1560 work based on Ovid, *The Fable of Ovid Treating of Narcissus* (London: Thomas Hackette).

The translation of Ovid's *Metamorphoses* published under Arthur Golding's name was the only English translation of that work until 1626. It was extremely popular in its day, going through eight editions since its first four books were published in 1565.

Ezra Pound, in *The ABC of Reading* (New Directions, 1934) called this translation "the most beautiful book in the [English] language," adding, "(my opinion and I suspect it was Shakespeare's) (58)." If only Pound had written "I suspect it was Shake-speare's translation," then I would be in complete agreement with him. Pound emphasized that "I do not honestly think that anyone can know anything about the art of lucid narrative in English…without seeing the whole of the [Golding] volume" (127). Pound is hyperbolic in his praise of this translation. In another essay, he calls Golding Ovid's equal. He goes on, "Is there one of us so good at his Latin, and so reading in imagination that Golding will not throw upon his mind shades and glamours inherent in the orginal text which had for all that escaped him?…it is certain that 'we'…have forgotten our Ovid since Golding went out of print" (*Literary Essays of Ezra Pound,* New York: New Directions, 1985, 235).

Pound is not the only critic who has strongly linked the Golding Ovid with Shakespeare. L.P. Wilkinson,[66] writes, "[Shakespeare] draws on every book of the [Golding] *Metamorphoses*, and there is scarcely a play that shows no trace of its influence" (410). Ovid's book is mentioned explicitly in *Titus Andronicus* IV.i. The context, interestingly enough, is the need to solve a puzzle of anonymity. Lavinia, the daughter of Titus Andronicus, has been raped, and her tongue and hands have been cut off so that she cannot name her rapists. As a first step toward communicating her plight, she looks through several books, and turns the pages of one book in particular. When Titus asks his grandson Lucius which book it is, he replies "Grandsire, 'tis Ovid's Metamorphosis,/ My mother gave it me" (l. 42-43). Lavinia turns the pages until she finds the story of the rape of Philomele, who also had her tongue cut off by her rapist, her sister's husband (Book VI, 526-909).

The unifying theme of Ovid's poem is transformation from one shape into another. The gods regularly transform people into animals, trees, and flowers. To quote the poem, "And aptly into any shape his persone he can shift" (XIII, l. 784). This is precisely what the young de Vere accomplished by allowing his uncle to sign de Vere's translation, and to use a variety of other allonyms and pseudonyms during his long literary career.

Several Oxfordians have already agreed that de Vere may well have been the translator of this work.[67] Among them are Charlton Ogburn (Jr.) (1984); Elisabeth Sears (*Spear-Shaker Review* 1(1):24-30, 1987); Robert R. Prechter (2007; *TOX* 10: 111-120); Paul H. Altrocchi (Xlibris2010); Hank Whittimore (2016); William J. Ray [wray.net];

In this extraordinary work of the fifteen-year-old de Vere (that is, the first four books), he seized the rhetorical figure of hendiadys he knew from reading Virgil. In addition, he probably read Johannes Susenbrotus's *Epitome Troporum ac Schematum*, published in London two years earlier. Susenbrotus was the first Renaissance writer to give a clear description of hendiadys.

Allow me to quote from an earlier essay (see Chapter Three)[68] to summarize George T. Wright's landmark study of hendiadys in Shakespeare—

Wright helped draw attention to the fact that Shake-speare used this figure of hendiadys more than 300 times.[69] Examples that have entered common use include "sound and fury," "slings and arrows," and "lean and hungry." Wright excludes from his use of the term what he derisively calls Shakespeare's "ceremonious parading of synonyms," that is, two closely related words, "without any significant increment, usually for an effect of expansion or elevation" (174). If we follow Wright in his derogation of insufficiently complex word pairs, we will deprive ourselves of taking the full measure of de Vere's lifelong fascination with word pairs, and the growth and development that his use of them underwent in his writing career. They tell us something important about his mind and spirit. One thing reminded him of another, and he linked them with a conjunction. One word alone often did not suffice, and in pairing it with a second, he drew a line that gestured toward meanings and connotations that went beyond mere words.

And Wright specifies that, as Shakespeare usually used the figure, "the parallel structure may mask some more complex and less easily describable dependent relation" between the two words (which are usually nouns in the later Shakespeare) (169). Further, classical hendiadys, including in Shakespeare, should have an "element of surprise, of improvisation, and of eccentric coordination" (171). Wright finds that hendiadys in Shakespeare "normally but not invariably occurs in passages of a certain elevation, dignity, or remoteness from ordinary experience" (173).

In addition to Susenbrotus, another important rhetorical treatise was by Johann Sturm, translated into English in 1570 as *A Ritch Storehouse or Treasurie for Nobilitie and Gentlemen*. In a previous publication, I have explained why I believe de Vere himself was the translator of this work. If so, it is telling that a word pair used three times in the *Metamorphoses*, "form and beauty," is also found in the Sturm translation ("the same did make the *forme and beautie* of the Goddesse"). When that hendiadys is used in Ovid, it is first put in the mouth of the goddess Venus; another time, it describes a nymph.

Gordon Braden writes compellingly of the Ovid translation attributed to Golding.[70] Inadvertently, he drops numerous hints that are more consistent with de Vere rather than Golding having been the actual translator. For example, he notes that Golding did not use as much hendiadys (which he calls "doublets") in his later works. But in "his" Ovid, "he often renders a single Latin word twice or more" (17). Braden implies that one source of the hendiadys in de Vere's Ovid is the translator's "habit of translating by multiple synonyms" (5). Every translator knows that there are often no exact equivalents between words of the two languages at issue, so the use of two words in English helps capture the Latin original. Italian offers the noun *sprezzatura*, from the verb *sprezzare*, "to distain." It is variously translated as non-chalance; or as effortless mastery. French offers *l'esprit d'escaliers*, which alludes to the witty come-back that only occurs to us too late, as we are walking down the stairs from the social event at which we were at a loss for words.

De Vere continued to use the figure of hendiadys throughout his literary career. Braden notes that "In *Midsummer Night's Dream* Shakespeare apparently quotes about half of one of Golding's lines almost verbatim" (p. 4): "a crowne of *fresh and fragrant* floures" in Ovid becomes "coronet of *fresh and fragrant* flowers" in the play (note the echoed hendiadys).

Braden ascribes youthful qualities to the translation: "In a simple and even naïve way Golding just wants to be easy to follow" (49). He says that the translator's attitude toward Ovid "is not sophisticated detachment but a deep, naïve intimidation" (54). The translation "is full of moments of quietly spreading astonishment…" (32). And "The quality of astonishment is *childlike*" (33; emphasis added). Braden is an honest scholar, and does not conceal these observations, despite their enhancing our sense that "Golding's connection with Ovid is often considered a matter for surprise and something of a puzzle" (9). Further, Braden perceptively links parallels between the "Golding" Ovid and the later works of "Shakespeare." Shake-speare understood Ovid's Latin better than did "Golding." I.e., the adult de Vere, compared with the teenaged de Vere. He says, "Reading Golding, we can trace the beginnings of a particular poetic world that Shakespeare twenty years later would bring to its fullest development" (36).

Caroline Spurgeon, in her classic study of Shakespeare's imagery, emphasizes his sympathy for all living creatures, even snails. Likewise, Braden notices that Golding and Shakespeare are similar in giving Ovid's bull (II, 1063) "a much more human kind of craftiness, a kind of false, indolent innocence" (4). Not actually similar, but coming from the same mind and personality, earlier and later in his writing career, respectively. Another stylistic parallel for Braden is Golding's "casual additions" to and "off-handed expansions" of Ovid's Latin; while "Decoration lightly borne is an important part of Shakespeare's poetics" (7). One thinks of de Vere's role in the publication of Castiglione's *The Perfect Courtier*, with its ideal of *sprezzatura*, or non-chalance. Braden admits that Golding "was, after all, a man closer to being [Shakspere's] social and cultural opposite than his fellow" (7). Braden then dismisses the Oxfordian authorship theory as created solely "by those embarrassed by [Shakspere's] low origins" (8). Ad hominem reasoning is dangerous, and here it leads Braden to ignore the abundant evidence for de Vere's authorship. Consequently, Braden fails to use his superb research and close reading to challenge the traditional authorship assumption.

Instead, Braden falls victim to the unconsciously circular thinking that plagues orthodox Shakespeare scholarship. He looks at the utter incongruity of a sincere Puritan such as Golding writing such a prurient translation, then concludes we do not really understand the Elizabethans. First, he points out that Calvin was Golding's favorite author to translate (what would Calvin have said about the *Metamorphoses*?). Further, "Moral didacticism, mixed with anti-Papist rhetoric, fills most of his prefaces—especially, with good reason, the dedications to the young Earl of Oxford [for whose translation of Ovid Golding was supposed to take credit]—and there is nothing in their tone or in what we know of Golding's life to suggest that he might not be serious" (p. 8).

Braden comments on the tone of Golding's 600-line dedicatory epistle, with its feeble claim that the translation is intended to warn the reader against immoral behavior. Braden then refers to the 222-line Preface, presuming it is also written by Golding. No, the lines that Braden quotes from the Preface openly mock the squeamish reader (before advising him to emulate Ulysses and be tied to the mast to resist temptation)—

"If any stomacke be so weake as that it cannot brooke,

The lively setting forth of things described in this booke,

I give him counsell too absteine untill he bee more strong"

(Preface, 215-217)

We might also look at the first two lines of the Preface, with its disingenuous "apology" to readers who resemble his uncle, Arthur Golding—

"I would not wish *the simple sort* offended for to bee,

When in this booke the heathen names of feyned Godds they see." (emphasis added)

This Preface sounds far more like the youthful de Vere, casting himself as physician whose patient is temporarily impaired by illness, and must recover before he can safely enjoy de Vere's translation. And his reference to the "simple sort" in the first line has many possible allusions to Puritans such as his uncle. At that time, "simple" could mean innocent and honest. But it could also signify common, or of low rank, and his uncle was far below de Vere in the social structure of the day. Recall the Puritans' aversion to fine clothing as you consider that "simple" could also mean wearing attire that lacks elegance. "Simple" likewise meant weak or feeble, anticipating the three lines quoted above about a "weake" stomacke that needs to become "more strong." "Simple" could further mean intellectually deficient, as it still does today. One can imagine de Vere's exasperated uncle reading the manuscript of de Vere's translation, then imploring his nephew to write a preface that would pacify potentially offended readers. With what was later called de Vere's "perverse temperament," he instead chose to mock unappreciative readers, perhaps especially the Puritans.

Hamlet famously advised the actors that the purpose of theater is to hold a mirror up to nature. De Vere used a strikingly similar image in his Preface, to justify the book's detailed description of pagan sins—
"Now when thou readst of God or man, in stone, in beast, or tree
It is a myrrour for thy self thyne owne estate to see" (lines 81-82; emphasis added)[71]

The pattern of hendiadys itself helps attribute this Preface to de Vere. It contains the greatest concentration of hendiadys in the entire work. An average of 27% of its lines contain a word pair—that is, an average of once every four lines. Books I through IV, published in 1565, have hendiadys an average of every ten lines (or 10% of their lines). Word pairs then drop off to 7% of the lines of Book V; 5-6% of the lines of Books VI and VII; then 2-3% of the lines of Books VIII through XIV. It is only in the final book that their occurrence picks up to 5% of the lines, for Book XV. To the extent that his use of this rhetorical figure revealed de Vere's youthful creative exuberance, he gave it fullest vent in the Preface; less so in the first four books; then he seemed to have a bit less creative energy for this device in the remainder of his translation (published and perhaps written two years later), getting his second wind for the final book.

Gordon Braden, only 31 when he published his book, says "Golding's most memorable intrusions of authorial comment are *not Puritan at all*, but show a very secular combination of impatience and amusement." (p. , emphasis added).This description is more consistent with the 17-year-old de Vere than with the Puritan Golding.

As do Braden's repeated descriptions of "childlike" and "naive" characteristics of the "Golding" Ovid. E.g., "The quality of astonishment is childlike..." "In a simple and even naive way Golding just wants to be easy to follow"; "...the bashfulness of his opening lines."

One thinks of de Vere as "E.K." in Spenser's A Sheepherd's Calendar when Braden observes of Golding's substantive additions to Ovid, "These are the intruded glosses, never allegorizing but merely explanatory in an antiquarian way."

Braden notes that Golding's approach "indicates a way of looking at everything, with interest, but no compulsion to interfere: a style of omniscience that sees all, knows all, and does not mind. We are in various ways close to the sensibility of the early Shakespeare comedies." Again, this is consistent with de Vere's authorship of both. Golding's "sense of humor that sometimes seems to go completely haywire" reminds one of Sidney Lee saying that de Vere's perverse sense of humor was a source of grave embarrassment to Lord Burghley.

Braden returns to the vast impact of the *Metamorphoses* on Shakespeare in a much later work.[72] He includes Shakespeare as one of the many Elizabethan writers who were deeply influenced by Ovid. His chapter focusses on Ovid's poems written in exile. De Vere, whom Queen Elizabeth exiled from court after de Vere impregnated Anne Vavasour, would have felt a special kinship with Ovid's exile for offending the Roman emperor. Braden then notes the special salience of allusions to Ovid in *The Tempest*. He likens Prospero's exile to that of Ovid. "Prospero found himself in the middle of nowhere because he was undone by his love of his books" (54). Drawing attention to a little-known detail, Braden adds that "Prospero sought his redemption in perfecting his mastery of the one book that was left to him…the imaginative guess at what that book is would be the Metamorphoses" (55). As Mary Douglas discovered, in "ring composition,"[73] the literary work returns to its beginning at the end. And so with de Vere's literary career. In the play that has been considered Shakespeare's farewell to the theater, de Vere, as Prospero, returns to his adolescent translation of Ovid. As Braden says,

> *The Tempest* is the capstone work of the Shakespearean corupus, his summing up of the power and nature of his theatrical craft. It seems appropriate that a centerpiece of this summing up would be the most extensive of his direct appropriations from Ovid that had characterized his writing almost from the beginning [indeed, from fifteen years old!]: this had always been his great book of magic… (p. 55)

We can be immensely grateful to Braden for his valuable help in elucidating the "Golding" Ovid. We can only regret he stopped short of connecting the dots he so perceptively identified.

Our name is central to our sense of identity. De Vere had been Viscount Bulbec since birth. Since twelve (three years before this the first four books of this translation were published), Edward de Vere also became Earl of Oxford[74] (as well as Lord Sanford and of Escales and Badlesmere), after his father died. So even his multiplying titles may have enlarged his sense of his complex identity, sensitizing him to the rich possibilities of word pairs.

He not only helped introduce it into English literature—he also explored its rich possibilities, including various ways of "doubling" the hendiadys twins. For example, his first use of this figure is a double one—"A *heavie lump and clottred* [clotted] *clod* of seedes togither driven" (I, line 8).

In one couplet he employs two consecutive, rhymed, double hendiadys, consisting of four adjectives modifying four nouns, joined by two conjunctions—
"I never was in *greater care nor more perplexitie,*

How to maintain my *soveraigne state and Princelie royaltie*" (I, 208-209).

I mention these examples because of their inherent interest. However, I will mostly restrict myself to conventional hendiadys in this work, rather than such atypical "doubled" forms.

Steven May, a Stratfordian expert on de Vere's signed poetry, calls his poetic style "highly experimental." Here, de Vere even experiments with enjambed hendiadys, with a line break between its two halves—
"More precious yet than freckled brasse, immediately the *olde*
And auncient Spring did Jove abridge, and made thereof anon,
Four seasons…" (I, 132-134).
As well as--
"Then to beholde: yet forbicause he saw the earth was *voyde*
And silent like a wildernesse, with *sad and weeping* eyes…" (I, 408-409).
In Book VIII (682-683), "…torne/ And tattred," combines enjambment with alliteration.

These line breaks encourage the reader not to treat the word pairs as closely related, by forcing us to pause between them, giving us time to ponder the nuances of each word's respective meaning. As noted earlier, this may prime the reader to read all hendiadys with greater care and attention. This pair of hendiadys is all the more arresting, as it is the unique use of "void and silent" in EEBO, and the first (of 18) of "sad and weeping."

The second half of hendiadys may amplify the first half, as in "with *sad and weeping* eyes" (I, 409). "Sad" is an emotional state visible in one's facial expression; "weeping" is a behavior that makes stronger and more concrete that emotional state of sadness. Both words come from old Saxon. Or "the *grim and greedy* Wolfe" (355), the first of two instances of that phrase in EEBO. Those two words both have an old Saxon origin. The last two examples are especially alliterative, beginning with the same two consonants (cl- and gr-). A single line has the doubly alliterative "dowles [boundary markers] and ditches," then "free and fertile" (I, 152). The first pair is unique in EEBO. Notice the play of "f" and "r" in that second pair, the first of two instances in EEBO. Not a hendiadys, but earlier the translator wrote, "The *fertile* earth as yet was *free*" (I, 115), thus echoing them 37 lines later. De Vere coins the alliterative "sort and sute" (Book IX, 109); only seven lines later, he adds the commonplace "sauf and sound," repeating the initial letters.

Alliterative hendiadys combines two of his stylistic devices. Examples abound: "meeke and meeld"; "fly and follow"; "fowle and filthye"; "wynd and weather"; "sword and spear"; "strives and strugles" (the same first *three* letters in each word).

De Vere is sometimes ridiculed for the seemingly excessive alliteration in his early signed poetry. One finds the same profusion of alliteration in this translation of Ovid. The "w" sound is repeated seven times in "The wonted weight was from the Waine, the which they well did wot" (Book II, l. 212). In case the inattentive reader missed this, three lines later one reads "Even so the Waine for want of weight it erst was wont to beare."

Alliterative hendiadys is especially pleasing to the ear, making a further connection between the two linked words. "Wyde and wynding" (Book IX, 24) is a unique hendiadys using two closely similar words. Alliteration combines with assonance in the unique "meate [flesh, or food in general] and mancheate [fine wheat bread, or food in general]" (Book X, 133). Further, there is implicit wordplay with the verb "eat" being contained in these two word for food.

"Unforct and unconstrainde" (I, 104) recalls Shakespeare's fondness for words beginning "un-"; he coined more than 300 such words in the canon. In this translation, de Vere coined fourteen such words (more on that later).

In this work, de Vere could go a few pages without using a single word pair, then use several within just a few verses. De Vere seemed to coin new hendiadys when a given image especially intrigued him—"the thicke and foggie ayre" (I, 22) is the first of 113 uses of "thick and foggy" in EEBO; forty lines later, de Vere coins the related "*mist* and cloudes" (I, 61), the first of 9 uses in EEBO. Fifteen lines later, he coins "shoures [showers] and rotten *mists*" (I, 76), elaborating on this same theme.

De Vere also composes verbal themes and variations with hendiadys. He speaks of "thicke and *muddie slime*" at line 436; it is the first of 115 uses of this word pair in EEBO. Only 60 lines later, he turns this into "fat and *slimie mud*" (I 498); the first of 17 uses of that word pair in EEBO. Two lines later, he has "*fat* and lively soyle" (I, 500), the first of only two uses of this hendiadys in EEBO. In the latter two phrases, one or two words are repeated from the prior phrase, whereas one or two new words are introduced. Readers with good verbal memories are rewarded, with the pleasure of déja entendu. Judicious repetition is inherent in good art.

Spending time with de Vere's hendiadys leads one to surmise that he did not regard similar words simply as synonyms. As when he repeats a single word in his plays because it has a different nuance each time, he is asking us to notice different shades of meaning in the words he pairs. He was the first to use "woods and forests" (I, 573).[75] It is easy to dismiss these words as mere synonyms. But, in de Vere's day, woods were usually smaller than forests; further, the latter referred specifically to royal hunting districts. The French etymology of the latter, in contrast with the Anglo-Saxon origin of "woods," underlined this difference between king and commoners.

Caroline Spurgeon notes that one of Shakespeare's favorite images was of the human body in motion. In Book One, de Vere writes of ships that did "leap and daunce" (151); and he says that Phaeton began "to leap and skip for joy" (984).

Some examples have a parallel construction, with the same word modifying both halves of the word pair. E.g.,
"But one of eche, howbeit those *both just and both devout*" (I, 383).

I count 20 instances of hendiadys in Book I of Ovid that are unique in EEBO. That is one measure of the prominence of this figure. Another measure is when a given example is the first instance, followed by other writers who used (or borrowed?) the same word pair. Of these, I count 35 examples in Book I. Anywhere from one to 200 subsequent examples of that hendiadys are found in EEBO. Again, this is merely in the first of 15 sections of the *Metamorphoses*.

On the first page of his preface, de Vere uses six word pairs in only two line—

"Of *health and sicknesse, lyfe and death*, of *needinesse and wealth*,

Of *peace and warre*, of *love and hate*, of murder, *craft and stealth*."

This profusion of hendiadys (unique in the book) anticipates the stylistic plenitude of de Vere's later euphuistic phase, characterized by verbal superabundance (captured in *Loves Labor Lost*).

In Book VIII (682-683) , "The Lords and Commons did lament, and maried wives with *torne/ And tattred* haire did cry alas…" combining enjambment with alliteration.

These line breaks encourage the reader not to treat the word pairs as closely related, by forcing us to pause between them, giving us time to ponder the nuances of each word's respective meaning. This may prime the reader to read all hendiadys with greater care and attention. This pair of hendiadys is all the more arrresting, as it is the unique use of "void and silent" in EEBO, and the first (of 18) of "sad and weeping."

The second half of hendiadys may amplify the first half, as in "with *sad and weeping* eyes" (409). "Sad" is an emotional state visible in one's facial expression; "weeping" is a behavior that makes stronger and more concrete that emotional state of sadness. Both words come from old Saxon.

As noted earlier, de Vere coined some 390 hendiadys in this work, including its Preface. Some 230 word pairs are apparently first used in this work, and then used by subsequent writers. An additional 160 of the word pairs are unique, at least in EEBO. Naturally, these examples are of special interest. In Book XV, l.527 we find "away with *Risp and net.*" "Risp" is first found in EEBO in 1553; the present example is only its second use. It refers to a bush used to trap birds. In 1553, it was used in a translation of Virgil's *Aeneid* into "Scottish meter," coincidentally by Gawin Douglas, another uncle of an earl (the Earl of Angus). De Vere was constantly enlarging the English language, which may have been one of his motives in linking "risp" with "net" here.

Spending time with de Vere's hendiadys leads one to surmise that he did not regard similar words simply as synonyms. As when he repeats a single word in his plays, he is asking us to notice different shades of meaning in the words he pairs. He was the first to use "woods and forests" (573).[76] It is easy to dismiss these words as mere synonyms. But, in de Vere's day, woods were usually smaller than forests; further, the latter referred specifically to royal hunting districts. The French etymology of the latter, in contrast with the Anglo-Saxon origin of "woods," underlined this difference between king and commoners.

De Vere is recognized as the leader of the Euphuists. And his early use of hendiadys exemplifies the verbal exuberance of euphuism.

Using one hendiadys often led de Vere to use others in succeeding lines, or even in the same line. This may reflect what cognitive psychology calls "priming." In a single line of his Preface (l. 123) he coins two contiguous hendiadys—

"Even so a *playne and naked tale or storie* simply told…"

Book IV (808-810) has three original hendiadys in only three consecutive lines:
"As *huge and big* as Atlas was he tourned in that stead
Into a mountain: into trees his *beard and locks* did passe:
His *hands and shoulders* made the ridge…"

Book XV, lines 910-912 also includes three original hendiadys in three consecutive lines:
"Doo dwell, thou shouldest there of *brasse and steele* substantiall see
The registers of things so *strong and massye* made to bee,
That *sauf and everlasting*, they doo neyther stand in feare…"
In each of these six cases, the word pairs are used many more times in EEBO.

These three word pairs constitute a continuation of an image of something so strong that it will endure. The repetition carries emphasis. According to EEBO, these word pairs are the first of 34; of 20; and of 2 uses, respectively. The first hendiadys anticipates Sonnet 120, l. 4:
"Unless my nerves were *brass* or hammer'd *steel*"

There are several examples here of a hendiadys first used in a translation of the works of Erasmus. E.g., Book XV, 932 has "the wyld and barbrous nacions"; in 1537 translation of Erasmus's *Declamation*, the translator uses that very phrase, "the wylde and barbarous nacions." "Sharp and eager," used first in a 1548 translation of Erasmus, is used for the second time here. Thus, one strongly suspects the young de Vere read Erasmus, a foremost Renaissance humanist.

The Psalms, which were a major literary influence on Shakespeare, regularly use repetition for emphasis, and this is one effect of de Vere's hendiadys. They also have the effect of slowing down the pace of his poem, as it pauses to intensify a point.

Rhymed hendiadys are pleasing. Book XIII includes "quake and shake" for the first time; it was used in 40 subsequent works, including by Ben Jonson.

One hesitates to say it, but there is an example of a triple "hendiadys" in Book XIII, l. 146: "But myne [shield] is *gasht and hakt and stricken* thurrough quyght."

Conversely, when the Ovid translation is the first instance of a given word pair, learning who used it afterwards may be a clue that they read this translation (or wrote it!). For example, it includes the first use of "spade and mattock" (Book XI, l. 880). That phrase later appears in Shakespeare's *Romeo and Juliet*. Two lines earlier in Ovid is the first use of "fair and sheene [beautiful]"; the second use of that hendiadys is in Spenser's *Faerie Queene*.

What about hendiadys in the Medea speech in Book Seven that Prospero alludes to in Act V, scene one of *The Tempest*?[77] Again, four examples of newly coined (but later echoed) hendiadys: "Charmes and Witchcraft," "herbe and weed," "Ayres and windes," and "raise and lay." "Woods and forests" reappears after being coined in Book One, and "stones and trees" is used for the second of 105 instances in EEBO.

In Book 15, there is the 12th instance of "hands and eyes" in EEBO. What's striking about it is that the 11th instance is in Arthur Brookes' Romeus & Juliet. The context is similar: in Brookes, "With handes and eyes heaved up/he thanks God." In Ovid, "to heaven he cast his handes and eyes."

Shakespeare is said to have coined more than 300 words beginning "un-". Remarkably, this translation coins fourteen such words: unreele; unfrayd; unambicious; unsurmysed; unastaunched; unsentfor; unavoyded; unwish; unhated; unwieldsome; unfaded; unbetrayed; unhackt [the OED incorrectly lists Shakespeare's *King John* as having coined the word]; and unappeasd [once again, the OED erroneously credits Shakespeare with coining this word years later, in *Titus Andronicus*]. This fact alone increases the likelihood that "Shakespeare" translated this work.

In addition, there are other verbal "fingerprints" of de Vere in this translation. Book Six, lines 269-70, rhyme "naamde" with "ashaamde." The first spelling appears only one other time in all of EEBO; the second not another single time. And who do we know who had a quirky way of doubling his vowels in his letters? As in "caald," "caale," "faale," "haales," and "waales." None of those idiosyncratic vowel doublings appear a single time in EEBO. But that's how de Vere sometimes spelled those words in his surviving letters. Quaakt (4 times), shaakt (3 times), inflaamd (3 times), spaakst, maakst, prepaarde, daarde, raazd, and blaazd appear only in this translation--nowhere else among the 50,000 or so fully searchable books on EEBO. So in de Vere's letters, and in the "Golding" Ovid, we find "aa" spellings that are not found at all, or not found elswhere, respectively, in EEBO.

Yes, Elizabethan spellings were variable. Yes, we can argue that compositors chose the spellings, or that de Vere dictated his letters to his secretary. (Or that his secretary later worked as a compositor, I suppose.) Alan Nelson, who is regarded as a competent paleographer, takes de Vere to be the person who wrote his own letters. That's why he emphasizes de Vere's quirky spellings so much, without realizing how much he has thereby helped our case.

W.H. D. Rouse, in his 1904 edition of "Golding," noted that in the second complete edition of 1575, spellings are changed from the more regular forms on 1567 to more, well, quirky ones. Many more double vowels, which de Vere favored in his letters. And Rouse singled out the following quirky spellings in the 1575 edition: *bin, blud, death, heare, hart*, and *hir*. *All* of these spellings may be found in de Vere's extant letters. So it is possible that de Vere, now 25 years old, exerted more control over such matters in the 1575 edition, whereas his uncle edited his idiosyncratic (and often antiquated) spellings in the 1567 edition.

There are numerous instances of Shakespeare echoing Ovid's word pair, with the two words in close proximity to each other. Yes, there is no doubt that this translation was one of Shakespeare's most significant literary sources. But this pattern of echoes--reminiscent of Carl Jung's word association test to assess the uniquesness of each personality--further suggests a similar process of verbal association in the mind of the translator and the author of Shakespeare. Below, I list some examples.

As noted earlier, the Preface has a higher concentration of hendiadys than the rest of the book—61 examples in only 222 lines. This should resolve the question of whether the incidence of hendiadys in the rest of the translation is merely due to their presence in Ovid's original Latin. The Preface has the unique hendiadys "trees and stones," while Lorenzo in *Merchant of Venice* (V.i) says "Orpheus drew *trees, stone*s and floods." Similarly, it includes the unique strange and monstrous," while Quince in *Midsummer Night's Dream* says "O *monstrous*! O *strange*!" Note that one italicized word brings the other to mind for both translator and playwright—further evidence that they are one and the same writer.

Book I (line 101) includes EEBO's unique "shape nor hew." The title character of *Hamlet* (V.ii) verbs these two nouns in "There's a divinity that *shapes* our ends,/ Rough-*hew* them how we will."

Book I (125) has the first of EEBO's 47 instances of "lean and barren." *Venus and Adonis* (156) has "Thick-sighted, *barren, lean…*"

Book II (301) describes the Aethiopians as "black and swart." That is the first of 15 uses of that word pair in EEBO. Joan la Pucelle, in 1 Henry VI (I.ii) says "I was *black and swart* before." Book II (1016) also includes the first of 38 EEBO examples of the hendiadys "light nor heate." In *Hamlet* (I.iii), Polonius says "Giving more *light* than *heat*." (960) has the first of 26 EEBO uses of "Snakes and Todes." Tamora, in *Titus Andronicus* (II.iii) speaks of "a thousand hissing *snakes*,/ Ten thousand swelling *toads*."

Cadmus is described in Book III (7) as "kinde and cruell." In *Hamlet* (III.iv), the title character famously says "I must be *cruel*, only to be *kind*." Book III (272) includes "*over hill and dale*." That is the second EEBO instance of this hendiadys; the first was by de Vere's uncle Henry Howard, in his 1557 *Songes and Sonettes*. The Fairy in *Midsummer Night's Dream* (II.i. 369) sings nearly the same phrase in "*Over hill*, over *dale*."

Book IV includes the hendiadys used for the first time here, and borrowed the most often subsequently: 857 further instances of it are found in EEBO. It is "That *heart and hand* and all did faile in working for a space" (212). I Henry VI (I.ii) has "My *heart and hand*s." *Troilus and Cressida* (IV.v) also includes "His *heart and hand*." *Coriolanus* (I.x) includes "Wash my fierce *hand* in's *heart*." Book IV also contains the first of 42 EEBO examples of "neat and trim." In *1 Henry IV* (I.iii), someone is described as "*neat*, and *trim*ly dress'd."

Book V (42) has the first of 59 EEBO uses of "powre and sway." Sonnet 65 (l. 2) is "But sad mortality o'er-*sways* their *power*."

Book VI has the first of 46 instances in EEBO of "haaste and speed." Shakespeare associates these seemingly redundant words in *Measure for Measure* (III.i): "*Haste* you *speed*ily." And in *Richard III* (III.i): "make all the *speedy haste* you may." In all instances, there is an implicit allusion to and contrast with the Latin adage, "festina lente," meaning "make haste slowly."

Book VII has EEBO's first of 45 instances of "heavie and unwieldie." *Romeo and Juliet* (II.v) has "*Unwieldy*, slow, *heavy*…" And *Richard II* has "I give this heavy *weight* from off my head/ And this *unwieldy* sceptre from my hand." Book VII also has the first of 50 instances in EEBO of "bones and dust." These words are connected in Sonnet 32 (l. 2): "When that churl Death my *bones* with *dust* shall cover." And *Titus Andronicus* (V.ii) has "I will grind your *bones* to *dust*."

In Book X, we find the first of 40 uses of "shape and nature" in EEBO; *Twelfth Night* has "the *shape* of *nature*" (I.v); *Pericles* has "*Nature*'s own *shape*" (V.prologue). In addition, "blood and hart" is used for the first of 44 times; *Antony and Cleopatra* (V.i) has "*blood* of *heart*s."

Book XI includes the first of 43 instances of "spade and mattocke" in EEBO; Shakespeare's early play *Titus Andronicus* includes "Tis you must dig with *mattock* and with *spade*" (IV.iii). And *Romeo and Juliet* includes "We took this *mattock* and this *spade* from him" (V.iii). It also includes the first of nine uses of "charge and break"; *Cymbeline* (III.iv) says "if sleep *charge* nature,/ To *break* it with a fearful dream…"

In Book XII alone, I found no notable instances of Shakespeare later associating the same words that were first used in a hendiadys here.

Book XIII has the first of 40 EEBO uses of "quake and shake." *Venus and Adonis* has Venus say that her heart, "like an earth*quake, shake*s thee on my breast."

Book XIV includes the first instance in EEBO of "heate and lyght"; it is the first of 400 uses. *Hamlet* includes "Giving more *light* than *heat*" (I.3.605).

Book XV has more unique hendiadys since Book X, and even more first instances that were later used by other writers. Among the latter is "harsh and hard," the first of 99 instances. In Troilus and Cressida we find "The cygnet's down is *harsh* and spirit of sense/ *Hard* as the palm of ploughman" (I.i.88-89).

Book VIII twice mentions a "boarspeare" (lines 459 and 553). It is the first instance of this word in EEBO (though the OED gives a usage in 1465). So the word was unusual in 1567. But we know the boar was de Vere's heraldic animal. When Rosalind and Celia in *AYLI* are discussing how to disguise their real identities with "poor and mean attire" and new names, Rosalind proposes to carry a "boar-spear." This is one of two times that word is used in Shakespeare. The other time is in *Richard III*, which was published in 1597, a year before the first play that carried the name "William Shakespeare" (but after *Venus and Adonis* and *Lucrece*, which used that pseudonym). So did "boar-spear" hint at the connection between de Vere and "Shakespeare"? I wonder.

In conclusion, I have used converging lines of evidence to strengthen past attributions of the "Golding" translation of Ovid's *Metamorphoses* to the precocious adolescent literary genius, Edward de Vere. It uses nine words with unusual "aa" spelling that appear nowhere else in EEBO; this is consistent with the five "aa" words in de Vere's surviving letters that do not appear at all in EEBO. Its fourteen coined words beginning "un-" are consistent with Shake-speare coining over 300 such words. And its 280 coined word pairs are consistent with Wright's estimate that Shake-speare coined more than 300 examples of hendiadys.

Why does it matter if de Vere translated Ovid's *Metamorphoses*? Among many other important reasons, perhaps the most salient is that it helps give us a more realistic picture of the maturation of literary genius from that of a precocious child to Shake-speare's mature works. Among the most implausible features of the traditional Stratfordian authorship theory is the implication that Shakespeare began writing at the height of his powers, with no developmental trajectory. De Vere's translation of Ovid helps refute this fanciful but foundational misconception of how Shake-speare's literary genius developed.

In subsequent chapters, I will examine a 1569 poem signed "A.G.," and explain in detail why I believe de Vere wrote it, and used his uncle's initials to imply it was by Arthur Golding. I will also show why a 1570 translation of a work on rhetoric by Johann Sturm was also written by de Vere. In particular, that chapter explores in further detail the multiple meanings of de Vere's use of hendiadys, which later comes into full flower in the works of "Shake-speare."

Chapter Two

A 1569 Poem, Newly Attributed to Edward de Vere[78]

 Rebecca Tomlin of Birbeck College published an article titled "A New Poem by Arthur Golding?" in the December 2012 *Notes & Queries* (59:501-505). In it, she speculates that a 1569 commendatory poem published above the initials "A.G." may have been written by Arthur Golding. Curiously, it commends a book by James Peele[79] on double-entry book-keeping. Tomlin links Golding's possible interest in this seemingly esoteric topic with his role as receiver to his nephew Edward de Vere, inheritor of vast estates. And Oxfordians speculate that the young de Vere may have at least collaborated with his uncle Arthur on the translation of Ovid's *Metamorphoses* published in 1567 (as I explained in the previous chapter, I believe de Vere was its sole translator). Further, the annotations in de Vere's Geneva Bible show his special interest in numbers, which de Vere often underlined, and sometimes copied in the margin as they appeared in the biblical text.

The poem is an acrostic, the first letters of each couplet (except the final three) spelling out Peele's name (as 'IACOBUS PEELE,' which is printed vertically to the left of the poem). It is written in the 'fourteeners' of the *Metamorphoses*. Tomlin finds its style to be similar to the *Metamorphoses* translation attributed to Golding. Oxfordians maintain that the Puritan Golding's precocious nephew was the actual translator, given the facts that the translation is even racier than Ovid's original; that the adolescent de Vere's Puritan guardian William Cecil may not have allowed him to put his name to such a work; that Golding published nothing else like the *Metamorphoses*; and that Gabriel Harvey praised de Vere's apparently lost Latin poetry. If de Vere put his uncle's name to his translation of Ovid, it would be consistent to do the same with this 1569 poem.

There are some striking similarities between this poem and de Vere's other poetry. In both the 1569 poem and then again in de Vere's commendatory poem "To the Reader" in Thomas Bedingfields's 1573 translation of *Cardanus's Comfort*, the poet enlists the trope of the farmer laboring in the field to describe the work of the writer whose book is being celebrated. The 1569 poem says that "...every man (that will) may *reape* a *fruitefull harvest* heare:/ So *fertile* are these fields..."Then, in the next line, "As he *that tills* them." Four years later, de Vere's prefatory poem to *Cardanus's Comfort* begins, "The labouring *man, that tills* the *fertile* soyle/ And *reaps* the *harvest fruit*..." In his copy of the Geneva Bible, de Vere showed his unusual interest in *2 Esdras* 15:13 by annotating it in several ways. He underlined the verse number and several words; he drew five vertical dots in the left margin next to this verse; and he drew a pointing hand (manicule) next to it. It was rare for him to draw manicules in his Geneva Bible—he drew them mostly in his *Whole Book of Psalms*, bound at the end of it. The verse reads, "The plowemen that till the grounde, shal mourne: for their sedes shal faile thorowe [through] the blasting and haile, and by an horrible starre." In the Bible verse, the ploughmen work in vain. The context is God's promise to punish the Egyptians for their mistreatment of God's Chosen People.

Caroline Spurgeon[80] notes Shakespeare's fondness for snail imagery. In Chapter Four, I attribute an anonymous 1585 poem, "In Praise of Snayle," to de Vere. The 1569 poem also includes a snail trope: "...none/ Is borne by nature, like a *Snayle* to *live* at *home* alone." In speaking of the snail, the 1585 poem includes some of the same words: "that *lives* devoid of ease" and "to keep a quiet *home*."

As Tomlin observes, "'A.G.' adopts and adapts Golding's [i.e., the translator of Ovid, probably de Vere himself] description of the Labyrinth [of Daedalus] as a metaphor for the disorder of badly kept accounts... 'A.G.'s verse echoes Golding's distinctive phrasing and vocabulary" (502). For example, in the use of "busy" meaning intricate or impenetrable; and "clew" meaning a ball of thread that can guide one out of a maze. *Alls Well That Ends Well* uses "clew" to mean thread, as does Florio's translation of Montaigne's *Essays*. *Timon of Athens* coins "unclew," meaning to unwind, undo, or ruin.

Tomlin makes the crucial observation that the author of the 1569 poem may have been drawn to Peele's book because of his interest in "proper accounting as a means of ensuring moral rectitude and justice" (504). Paula Blank, in her 2006 *Shakespeare and the Mismeasure of Renaissance Man* made the intriguing observation that Shakespeare deeply considered every available means of measurement to ask if they might help in the moral appraisal of mankind. This 1569 poem suggests that this was an interest that had its roots in de Vere's adolescence.

It is noteworthy that some of the spellings in the 1569 poem are consistent with the unusual spelling variants that Alan Nelson found in de Vere's extant letters.[81] True, spelling was not yet normalized in the Elizabethan era. Yet de Vere went far beyond other Elizabethan writers in his love of variety in his spelling, spelling "half-penny" eleven different ways; as well as in his fondness for already antiquated spellings (e.g., "yow" for "you" and "owt" for "out"). Although Nelson, who wrote a (highly and negatively biased) biography believes that de Vere's idiosyncratic spelling habits disqualify him from having written the canon, they are consistent with some of the unusual spellings in Hand D of the manuscript of *Sir Thomas More*, where "country" is spelled three ways, and "sheriff" is spelled five different ways. Hand D has been definitively attributed to Shakespeare by some scholars, in the absence of any samples of the handwriting of William Shakspere of Stratford. The six extant signatures are so different from each other that is is unlikely they are by the same person. (Naturally, we do not know just how much control de Vere had over the compositors who set the type of his publications.)

What follows are some examples of similar spelling variants in the 1569 poem, de Vere's letters, and the 1567 *Metamorphoses*; all spellings of the words listed in EEBO for books published the same year as the 1569 poem are also given, for comparison.

For each word, I *first* give the spelling in the 1569 poem under discussion; *secondly*, the number ("x") of the various spellings ("vs.") of that word in de Vere's extant letters; *thirdly*, the number of times the various spellings were used in all books published in 1569 that are listed in EEBO; *fourthly*, I give the number of spellings of those same words in the 1567 edition of Ovid's *Metamorphoses* that may have been translated by the young de Vere. Despite how tedious such a comparison may be, it is among the many pieces of circumstantial evidence that strongly favor de Vere's authorship of this 1569 poem. Simultaneously, it is consistent with de Vere's authorship of the 1567 translation of Ovid's *Metamorphoses*. A similar methodology is helpful in comparing the spelling in early editions of the Shakespeare canon with spellings of the same words in de Vere's letters and signed works.[82]

De Vere's Spelling "Fingerprints" in this 1569 Poem

clayme; clayme/s 4x vs. claim/e 0 x; claym/e 12x vs. claim/e 21x; claym/e 5x vs. claim/e 1x

dew (meaning due); dwe 4x vs. due 1x; dew 32x vs. due 132x; dew 4x vs. due 9x

mynd; mynd/e 15x vs. mind/e 4x; mynd/e 186x vs. mind/e 854x; mynd/e 67x vs. mind/e 35x

neyther; neyther 8x vs. neither 0 x; neyther 0 x vs. neither 548x; neyther 98x vs. neither 10x

owt; owt 55x vs. out 15x; owt 1x vs. out 2,333x; owt 1x vs. out/e 282x

trew; trwe 17x vs. tru 1x vs. trew 0 x; trew 31x vs. true 997x; trew 14x vs. true 19x

vew; vew 1x vs. view 0 x; vew 13x vs. view 25x; vew 6x vs. view 4x

In other words, the variant spellings in the 1569 poem are highly consistent with de Vere's spelling in his letters and with the 1567 translation of Ovid's *Metamorphoses*, but moderately to extremely unusual for all of the (searchable) books on Early English Books Online (EEBO) that were published in 1569. Most extreme is "owt" in the 1569 poem, a spelling which de Vere used 55 times in his letters (whereas he used "out" only 15 times); "owt" was used only once in the 1569 searchable EEBO books, compared with 2,333 instances of "out."[83] Similarly, the 1569 poem uses "trew," whereas the 1569 books in EEBO used "true" 32 times as often as "trew"; but de Vere's letters use the unusual "trwe" spelling 17 times, but "tru" only once. By contrast, "claym/e" and "vew" are spellings that are both found in the 1569 poem and in de Vere's letters; the latter used only those spellings for those two words. But these two spellings were used roughly half as often as "claim/e" and "view," respectively, among the same sample of 1569 books.

Although these striking similarities are not conclusive proof, they are consistent with de Vere's authorship of the 1569 poem. We should not ignore the possibility that de Vere cared enough about his literary works to dictate precise spellings to his compositors. His reputation for having killed a servant at 17 may have made his compositors more cooperative with this tempermental nobleman's quirky spelling preferences.[84]

Not for the first time, a Stratfordian scholar (Rebecca Tomlin) has inadvertently helped Oxfordian scholarship—this time, by drawing attention to a poem de Vere is likely to have written, and published when he was nineteen.

1569 Poem Newly Attributed Edward de Vere

TO THE READER in commendation of this present woorke.

In yelding every wyght his owne, trew justice doth consist,
the Gordian knot of manes estate[85] which no man can
untwist.[86]
A blissfull braunche wherof behold presented in this
booke,
whose fruite is pleasaunt for to tast[87] and wholesome for to
brooke.
Conveyance wrought by crafty flightes this touchstone
doth bewray.
This lampe bringes open light to thinges that deepe in
darkenes lay.
Of Rekninges buzyer than the *Maze* of *Dedalus*, this Clew
doth wynd men owt.[88] Greate thanks of you o
merchantmen are dew.
But what? Extendes this woorke alone to Merchauntmens
behoof?
and not to all men else that list to put the same in proof?
Upon advysed vew (no doubt) it plainly will appeare,
that every man (that will) may reape a fruitefull harvest
heare:
So fertile are these feeldes.[89] Which yelde so much the
greater gayne.
As he that tilles them greater trades of dealings doth
maintayne.
Peruse this worthy worke then, pend by *Peeles* most
painefull[90] hand:
and learne by just and trew accompt thy state to
understand.
Enforce the selfe yet furthermore, and beare in mynd that
none
is borne by nature, like a Snayle[91] to live at home alone.
Eche servaunt, kinsman, freend, alye, eche straunger,
every wyght,
with whom thou dealst, (as deale thou must) clayme

faithfulness and right.

Lo heare wherby to mend thy skill, thy credit to preserve,
to win thee welth, to get thee friendes, thy common weale
to serve.

Exceeding, yea immortall thankes thou oughtst to yelde
therfore

what wyght so ere thou art whose neede is helped by this
store.

And specially with you that deale with great and long
accountes,

whose Rekninges oft are intricate, whose charge right farre
amountes

Above the common rate, on whom doth oftentimes depend
the weale and welfare, or decay of thousandes in the end:

In part of *Peeles* dew[92] recompence for penning of this
same,

Let neyther spyght abate his prayse,[93] nor time outweare
his fame.

FINIS.

Chapter Three

"Edward de Vere Translated the 1570 *A Ritch Storehouse or Treasurie for Nobilitie and Gentlemen* by Johann Sturm"[94]

Edward de Vere hid his authorship behind such pen names as William Shake-speare; Ignoto; Anomos; and E.K. It is likely that he also hid his authorship of a translation of Ovid's *Metamorphoses* behind the allonym of Golding, as well as a 1569 commendatory poem signed "A.G." (another "initialonym"?). Did he simply sponsor the publication of Bedingfield's translation into Latin of *Cardus Comfort*, or did de Vere do the translation himself? We do not know yet. We do have evidence from the secretary of the Earl of Essex that Essex asked Fulke Greville to allow him to sign a document written by Essex as "F.G."[95] Essex's motives included a wish not to appear too self-congratulatory in this, well, self-congratulatory account of his role in the 1596 battle of Cadiz. So here is valuable evidence of another earl using a veiled allonym. In his *Arte of English Poesie*, de Vere, writing anonymously, hinted that hidden authors may lie concealed behind the authorial names of other actual people: "I know very many notable gentlemen in the court that have…suffered [their work] to be published without their *own* names attached to it" (112; emphasis added).

The 1570 English translation of Johann Sturm's Latin *A Ritch Storehouse or Treasurie for Nobilitye and Gentlemen* is a small, octavo edition of merely 96 pages, published by Henrie Dunham in London. This was one of Sturm's few Latin works to be translated into the vernacular during the 16th century. The title page names the translator as "T.B.," and its dedicatory epistle is signed "Thomas Browne." But I will present multiple lines of evidence suggesting that Edward de Vere was its actual translator.

Colin Burrow, in his survey of Shakespeare's relationship with the Latin classics, speculates that this very book by Sturm "is just the kind of aspirational work which Shakespeare might have *read*" (26; emphasis added). He surmises that "Shakespeare may have known *A Rich Storehouse* as early as the mid 1590s, since T.W. Baldwin notes an 'amusing parallel' between Holoferne's use of the word 'peregrinate' to describe an imported word and Sturm's treatise". Burrow adds that Donna B. Hamilton discussed the relationship of *The Tempest* with the same treatise (250 n. 8).

Elsewhere, Burrow writes,

"A tiny clue in the text of *Troilus* may also indicate that Shakespeare had recently read and thought afresh about the theory and practice of literary imitation. Hector makes a famously anachronistic comment that his brothers have spoken like 'young men, who Aristotle thought/ Unfit to hear moral philosophy' (2.2.166-7). Aristotle (4th century BC) could not have been read by a Homeric hero who was fighting at Troy during the Bronze Age...Shakespeare's error could have come from a number of sources, but one possibility is Johann Sturm's *Nobilitas Literata* (1549), which was translated into English in 1570 as *A Rich Storehouse or Treasure for Nobilitye and Gentlemen*. This includes an extended discussion of how one author should imitate another, in the course of which Sturm declares that imitation is not a childish activity, but is indeed suitable only for grown-ups: 'as Aristotle did exclude young boys from his *Ethics*: so I also remove from this artificial practice [of imitation] not only children and boys, but also those men which know not the precepts of rhetoric.' That embeds Aristotle's remark in a rhetorical setting that fits the formal *disputatio* between Hector and Troilus in 2.2. Sturm was an unusually enthusiastic advocate of a kind of imitation that has been called 'dissimulative,' in which 'an imitator must hide all similitude and likeness'" (608).[96]

So translating Sturm may have provided de Vere with further encouragement for continuing his "dissimulative" practice of hiding his authorship of most of his literary works.

We do know something of de Vere's relationship with Johann Sturm (1507-1589). De Vere thought so highly of him that he went out of his way to visit him in Strasbourg during his 14-month trip to the Continent in 1575-76. De Vere and Sturm were part of a network of eminent people in England and on the Continent. Sturm's friends included John Calvin, Andreas Vesalius, and Guillaume Budé. His former student Petrus Ramus became a renowned logician. Queen Elizabeth's tutor Roger Ascham was so friendly with Sturm that he named a son Johannes Sturm Ascham, and he corresponded with Sturm for 18 years. The Queen herself also greatly admired Sturm's work. A 1590 edition of poems in Sturm's honor was dedicated to Queen Elizabeth. Sturm wrote to Roger Ascham in 1551, praising the learning of some English noblemen. Spitz and Tinsley report that Ascham "was a devoted disciple of Sturm's educational and humanist writings."[97] Anderson notes that one of de Vere's servants said he "had a most high opinion" of Sturm. Sturm staunchly defended the French Protestants, harming himself financially through large loans to their cause. He was a liberal, tolerant humanist, whose efforts to build bridges among the Lutherans and Calvinists eventually led to his losing his academic position. He devoted much of his life and many of his writings to education. We might recall that Edward de Vere's grandfather founded a grammar school at Earls Colne in Essex, and that de Vere served as guardian of that school, appointing its schoolmaster.[98]

This chapter will present evidence that the 20-year-old de Vere admired Sturm's 1549 treatise on rhetoric so much that he translated it from Latin to English, hiding his role behind that of "T.B.," ostensibly Thomas Browne.[99] What do we know of Thomas Browne? There is no consensus as to his identity. We have no other works that he published. The brief *ODNB* article on him, by L.G. Kelly, has virtually no sources of information about him other than this 1570 translation. The article begins, "Brown, Thomas (*fl.* 1570), translator, was a member of Lincoln's Inn. He was either the Thomas Brown admitted on 13 October 1562, or Thomas Brown of London, admitted on 6 August 1565. The second of these could have been 'Thomas Browne of London', admitted to the Inner Temple in November 1575. He was not one of the myriad Thomas Browns in the university lists." I am skeptical of these inferences, given Marcy North's important work on the prominent role of anonymous Elizabethan authorship. Scholars who write articles about obscure Elizabethan authors for the *ODNB* need to consider the possibility that some of these authorial names are pseudonyms (or alloynms).

The 1570 translation is dedicated to the 13-year-old Philip Howard (1557-1595), who then had the honorable title of Earl of Surrey. Under the circumstances, dedicating a work to the son of Thomas Howard in 1570 was a bold act, possibly hinting at disloyalty to the Queen. The more reckless the act, the more it increases the likelihood that de Vere was its perpetrator. Philip Howard's father, Thomas Howard, Duke of Norfolk (1538-1572), was de Vere's first cousin, descended from their grandfather, the 15th Earl of Oxford, through Howard's mother, Frances de Vere. Lord Howard fell under suspicion of treason when he pursued possible marriage with Mary Stuart, Queen of Scots. This placed him in a faction that was directly opposed to de Vere's guardian and future father-in-law, William Cecil. Howard was placed in the Tower from October, 1569 to August, 1570, then under house arrest in Howard House, London. He was finally executed for treason in June, 1572. Philip Howard himself was to spend the last ten years of his own life in the Tower, also for treason.

How important was rhetoric to de Vere? It was central to his vision of writing, whether in his private letters; in his prose works (most notably, in his *Arte of English Poesie*); in his poetry; and in his plays. Quentin Skinner's *Forensic Shakespeare* (OUP, 2014) shows that "over and over again, Shakespeare's characters follow to the letter the instructions of the rhetorical handbooks…The hidden pattern within the plays, their close dependence on the ancient art of rhetoric, was perhaps intended for his eyes only" (from review by David Wootton, *TLS*, December 12, 2014, pp. 3-5). In my review of Skinner's book, I wrote,

One of the many reasons that I find Skinner's book so fascinating is that it dovetails with the likelihood that de Vere wrote the 1589 *Arte of English Poesie*. As Skinner points out, its third part deals extensively with rhetoric, especially figures of speech. By the way, Angel Day's 1586 *The English Secretorie*, dedicated to de Vere, included marginal glosses highlighting rhetorical figures.[100] It is noteworthy that Day uses the word "coined" in the sense that de Vere seems to have coined it in 1570:[101] "Such odd coyned tearmes," referring to an example of a "preposterous and confused kind of writing." (39). Further, in 1592 Day seems to have been the second author, after de Vere in the *Arte*, to use the term "hendiadys" in English. In his 1592 edition, Day included a new section on rhetorical figures.

The hypothesis that de Vere wrote *The Arte of English Poesie* gains support from the connections between Quintilian and the Shakespeare canon, because the *Arte* twice mentions Quintilian by name. Recall that the Arte is only the sixth book in EEBO to cite Quintilian. In the second chapter of Book 3, de Vere recommends the use of figures of speech. In that context, he says "I have come to the Lord Keeper Sir Nicholas Bacon, & found him sitting in his gallery alone with the works of Quintilian before him, in deede he was a most eloquent man, and of rare learning and wisedome, as ever I knew England to breed" (224).[102] And, in chapter 9 of Book 3, the author says that "the learned orators and good grammarians among the Romans, as Cicero, Varro, Quintilian, and others, strained themselves to give the Greek words [for figures of speech] Latin names" (241). Further, according to editors Whigham and Rebhorn, the *Arte* uses some 70 of Quintilian's terms for figures of speech. In fact, La Rue Van Hook states that "Book III shows quite conclusively that it is Quintilian who is the chief source for the terminology" of rhetoric in the *Arte* (116).[103]

Skinner convincingly demonstrates that Shake-speare had a deep interest in and familiarity with rhetoric, even though past scholars overlooked his acquaintance with any books on that subject. Skinner shows that Shake-speare quotes from Cicero's rhetorical work *De inventione*; from *Rhetorica ad Herennium*; and that he cites Thomas Wilson's 1554 *Arte of Rhetorique*. Notably, Wilson received help with an earlier book from Sir Thomas Smith, Edward de Vere's later tutor. Skinner shows that past discussions of Shake-speare's rhetoric misleadingly place central emphasis on *elocutio* (including word-play), whereas Shake-speare's real interest was primarily in *inventio*. The 1570 book's epistle to the reader states the "wish that the vulgar speech of commending might be kept until some worthy matters were *invented*..." (emphasis added).

Why has de Vere's central interest in rhetoric been downplayed in the past? Perhaps because of the misleading implications of the traditional authorship theory, that portray Shake-speare as a relatively unschooled, native genius. Even Oxfordians have not escaped from the influence of this misconception, perhaps making us loathe to think of de Vere showing an intense interest in the rhetorical skills that underlay his works of literary genius. The image of an unschooled Shake-speare clashes with Skinner's description of Shake-speare working with treatises of rhetoric at the forefront of his mind, and possibly open on his desk. He contends that Shake-speare even draws attention to the role of artifice in his art.

If we accept Skinner's revised picture of Shake-speare—and I believe we should—it makes it all the more likely that he is the author of the anonymous 1589 *Arte of English Poesie*, and of the 1570 translation of Sturm. Among the many ways that the Sturm translation influenced de Vere's later *Arte* is the fact that Sturm wrote his treatise to the Werter brothers in the second person, just as de Vere later addressed much of the *Arte* to Queen Elizabeth in the second person. Both works emphasize that words can be misused to deceive. Both works use unusual drawings to schematize different structures in poetry.

David Wootton, in his review of Skinner, concludes that Shake-speare follows the rules of rhetoric "precisely because he was aware that that art could not deliver the proof that [courtroom] decisions of life and death required. There is something wrong with the rules themselves…Shakespeare's courtroom scenes show an author not enamoured of rhetoric, but frustrated by it" (p. 5). Yet the recognition that rhetoric could be used to deceive is central to Sturm, as it is to the *Arte*. In the translator's epistle to the reader, he speaks disparagingly of "painted wordes and smooth Rhetoricke," in contrast with "good and precious" matter. So we might instead say that Shake-speare's courtroom scenes demonstrate just how deeply familiar with rhetoric he was, not that he idealized it as a foolproof way of ascertaining the truth. After all, the ancient stoics were controversial because they trained their students to win arguments, whether or not their winning side was the truthful one.

Skinner emphasized that Shake-speare's primary interest in rhetoric is *inventio*. Coining new words is one well-known Shakespearean instance of *inventio*. *A Ritch Storehouse* coined, in fact, "to *coin* a word" in its introductory section, "To the friendly reader": "I of necessitie must either *coyne* newe wordes, the auncient already being employed on lewde and peradventure wicked matters…" (1; emphasis added). Note the translator's justification for coining this use of the verb "to coin," and other words, as something he is compelled to do. This is 19 years before the first example of the verb "coin" in this sense given in the OED. For our purposes, it is significant that this later 1589 use is in an anonymous work I have previously attributed to de Vere, the *Arte of English Poesie*.

"Unfyled" is here newly coined in the dedicatory letter in the sense of "unpolished, rude." The OED erroneously states that Spenser coined that meaning of "unfiled" in his 1590 *Faerie Queene*. But de Vere actually coined it 20 years earlier. The creative energy brimming in this 1570 work embodies de Vere's desire to make the English language suitable for great literature. He is saying, as it were, "anything Greek and Latin can do, English can do better!"

There are at least twelve other newly coined words in *A Ritch Storehouse*. He introduces the coinage "concauses" [co-operating causes] by adding "or joined causes." "Sensentence" looks like a misprint, but it may have been de Vere's attempt to English the Latin "sententia," meaning opinion or maxim. "Sensentence" actually appears three more times in EEBO, though it failed to make the cut for the OED. "Turquif[y]ing" is a coined word that flopped, never to be used again. It meant "transforming"; as early as 1560, "turkish" could be a verb meaning "to transform." Transformation of ancient texts into new works that imitate them in a disguised way was central to the humanist literary project.

Another coinage that never got off the ground was "captaynecke." It is de Vere's quirky translation of "virumque" in the opening words of the *Aeneid*. De Vere is here enacting the advice he gave two sentences earlier, that literary imitation should create in place of the original "a thing eyther as good or better" (40r). So he experimented with an English equivalent ("ecke," or "eke") to the Latin suffix "-que," both meaning "also." Virgil wrote "Arma virumque cano"; de Vere translates this, "of armes, and of a captaynecke I doe indite [meaning to write, to compose a tale]" (39v). "Peregrinity," borrowed from Latin and from Rabelais, means "foreignness." The translator indicates he is coining a word when he writes, "a certayne peregrinitie, *if I may so terme it*" (35r). The OED erroneously gives its first use as by G. Fletcher, in 1591. De Vere's younger sister Mary married Peregrine Bertie (1555-1601) in 1578. He lived in William Cecil's home as a teenager, so it is possible that de Vere had him in mind when he coined "peregrinity," especially because Bertie was named as an allusion to his Protestant parents' years living on the Continent during the reign of Queen Mary.

EEBO[104] gives *Ritch Storehouse* as the first use of "patavine" ("related to Padua"). "Counterchaunge" is also first used as the English word for the Greek rhetorical term "antimetabole" in this work. Its first use in EEBO is just three years earlier, in 1567, in the generic sense of "exchange of one thing for another." The OED incorrectly gives its first use as a term of rhetoric in the *Arte*. Naturally, it is significant that this translation of antimetabole appears in both works that I attribute to de Vere.

Both EEBO and the OED give the 1585 T. Washington translation of a French book as the first instance of "defiguration," but it was apparently coined fifteen years earlier, in *A Ritch Storehouse*. Spitz and Tinsley translate a passage as "sketches…let our drawings be called…schematisms" (150). De Vere translates it as "figurative draughts, or if I might so terme them, *defigurations*" (24r; emphasis added). De Vere also introduced the word "aposchematisms" into the English language, transliterating the Greek word used by Sturm. This coinage did not catch on--it is the only instance of it in EEBO. "Schematism," but *not* "aposchematism," *is* in the OED. "Whuzzing [wind]" is the first of only two uses of "whuzzing" in EEBO; "whuzz" appears in the OED as a spelling variant of "whiz."

A Ritch Storehouse also coined new phrases, not just new words. For example, "envious emulation" is the first of 31 uses of this phrase in EEBO. A prominent Elizabethan meaning of "envious" was "malicious" in general. So the phrase plays on emulation as not only a desire to equal another, but also rivalry, and a dislike of those who are superior.

One theme in *A Ritch Storehouse* is secrecy and disguise. G.W. Pigman observes, "Of all the theorists of imitation Sturm is the most insistent on dissimulation" (11)[105] The word "hidden" occurs six times in this work; "hide" four times; "hider" once; "hyding" once; "secret" four times; "cover" in the sense of conceal four times; "covertly" once. Most of these words allude to the need to imitate the style of a great writer, while concealing this imitation—

> "We must…follow these waies and rules that I have shewed: that nothing be done or placed without a cause: and *yet after such maner, that the common sorte may not perceive it.* For as it is to be wished that our speeche maye please all men, and as we ought speciallye to indevor to obtayne the same: so also we must take great heede, that Arte, and Imitation, and the similitude and likeness be not espied" (46r,v; emphasis added).

Court insiders knew of de Vere's literary activities, while "the common sort" were probably taken in by his use of anonymity, pseudonymity, and allonymity. Significantly, Sturm includes the Greek word κεκρυμμενον, or "hidden." But de Vere uses a triple repetition to signal the importance of this word for him, translating it as, "that is as much as hidden, close, or secret" (35v). If I am correct in concluding that de Vere disguised his translation of this work, all these passages would have spoken to his early--and also lifelong--authorial self-concealment. So this may be one of Sturm's more profound influences on de Vere's career.

As I have noted, this translation anticipates de Vere's 1589 *Arte of English Poesie*, his own extensive treatise on rhetoric. The word "figure" appears 10 times in *Ritch Storehouse*, and 87 times in the *Arte*, reflecting de Vere's close study of rhetorical figures. Sturm says of figuration, "the varietie of these bringeth delight & taketh away sasiety" (38r). "Sasiety" is the spelling here of "satiety." The former spelling occurs only one other time in EEBO, in 1579.

In the first three paragraphs of this work, "wit" is spelled three different ways: "wytte," "witte," and "wyt." Alan Nelson, a paleographer, has emphasized de Vere's pattern of spelling one word multiple ways, more than did his contemporaries. "Hand D" in the manuscript of *Sir Thomas More* is said to be that of Shakespeare. Hand D spells silence "scilens." De Vere similarly includes an "sc" in his spelling of "necescassarye" (sic).[106] *Ritch Storehouse* also misspells "unnecessary" as "unnessarie." Further, EEBO has no other instances of its quirky phrase "easiest and necessariest." It includes the word "apploying" for "applying"; this is the unique occurrence of the former spelling in EEBO.[107] The work includes "cowpling" for "coupling," "howres"[108] for "hours," and "pawse" for "pause." [109] De Vere usually preferred "owt" to "out" and "fowre" to "foure" in his letters, at a time when the former spellings had become unusual. It is helpful to recall that "w" stood for and was at the time sometimes printed with a double "v," and "v" and "u" were somewhat interchangeable. De Vere often doubled vowels at a time when most spelling had dropped one of them ("adoo" for "ado," etc.).

This translation twice uses the phrase "native soil," which is used 15 times in the "Golding" translation of Ovid that some Oxfordians attribute to de Vere. It had only been used a total of 17 times in EEBO works prior to 1567. And it was used seven times in the 1573 *Hundreth Sundrie Flowres*, which some Oxfordians also attribute to de Vere, rather than to George Gascoigne. The following chapter discusses a poem first published in 1585, that contains the same phrase in its first stanza; I also attribute that poem to de Vere.

Hendiadys in *A Ritch Storehouse*

We know that de Vere favored the Virgilian rhetorical figure of hendiadys ("one through two"), or two related words connected by a conjunction (usually "and"). The figure was never described by classical authors, but was first described by Susenbrotus, in 1562. In his 1589 *Arte of English Poesie*, de Vere wrote, "Ye have yet another manner of speech when ye will seem to make two of one not thereunto constrained, which we therefor call the Figure of Twins, the Greeks *hendiadys*" (261). The 1592 edition of Angel Day's *The English Secretorie*, dedicated to de Vere, defines "hendiadis" as follows: "when one thing of it selfe intire, is diversly laid open, as to say *On Iron and bit he champt*, for on the Iron bit he champt: And *part and proy* [prey] *we got*, for part of the proy: Also *by surge and sea we past*, for by surging sea wee past. This also is rather Poeticall then otherwise in use" (89).

It is fitting that de Vere was the first English author to describe hendiadys, and also the one who most employed it. De Vere often doubled plot elements of his sources, including through his frequent doubled plots, with high-born characters in one plot, and commoners in the echoing plot. Likening hendiadys to twins reminds us that Shakespeare's source for *The Comedy of Errors* included just one pair of twins, which de Vere doubled to two pairs of identical twins in his version of the play. A twin brother and a sister appear in *Twelfth Night*. The word "two" appears 574 times in Shakespeare;[110] "double" appears 82 times; "pair," 41 times; "twain" (two) 39 times. The basic metrical unit of de Vere's poetry was the two-syllable iamb, another instance of doubling. The Greek etymology of "hendiadys" as "one through two" is reflected in de Vere's poetry about love. Sonnet 36 begins, "Let me confess that we two must be twain ["two," or "a couple," but also "asunder, separate, estranged"],/ Although our undivided loves are one." "Let the bird of loudest lay," probably written about Queen Elizabeth's love for the Earl of Essex, after their deaths, includes the stanza, "So they lov'd, as love in twain/ Had the essence but in one;/ Two distincts, division none:/ Number[111] there in love was slain."

De Vere learned languages such as ancient Greek and Anglo-Saxon, that still retained the "dual number" of nouns and verbs, that existed in proto-Indoeuropean. There are traces of this old form in modern words such as "both," "either," and phrases such as "you two." The two words in the dual number were related, which may have provided another source of de Vere's interest in hendiadys.[112]

Hendiadys may also reflect de Vere's pivotal image of mirrors and mirroring.[113] Hamlet was speaking of the entirety of de Vere's literary work when he said the purpose of art is to hold a mirror up to nature. Early modern mirrors did not reflect the exact likeness of today's mirror; in that sense, one word in hendiadys roughly—but not precisely--mirrors its twin. In addition, a foundational, implicit word pair for Renaissance humanists such as Sturm and de Vere was "now and then"—the way the present can be informed and enriched by a deeper understanding of the classical past and its literature. Like other humanists, de Vere deliberately avoided simple imitation of classical models. Renaissance humanists consistently transformed[114] these classical models into their own creations. Their sense of time differed from that of their medieval predecessors, who felt they were essentially living in the same historical era as the ancient Romans and Greeks.

George T. Wright helped draw attention to the fact that Shake-speare used this figure of hendiadys more than 300 times.[115] Examples that have entered common use include "sound and fury," "slings and arrows," and "lean and hungry." Wright excludes from his use of the term what he derisively calls Shakespeare's "ceremonious parading of synonyms," that is, two closely related words, "without any significant increment, usually for an effect of expansion or elevation" (174). If we follow Wright in his derogation of insufficiently complex word pairs, we will deprive ourselves of taking the full measure of de Vere's lifelong fascination with word pairs, and the growth and development that his use of them underwent in his writing career. They tell us something important about his mind and spirit. One thing reminded him of another, and he linked them with a conjunction. One word alone often did not suffice, and in pairing it with a second, he drew a line that gestured toward meanings and connotations that went beyond mere words.

Wright does observe that, from the beginning, paired words are used "to give a feeling of elevation or complexity" (173), a description that is apt for *Ritch Storehouse*. What Wright considers true hendiadys, in its best examples, "make[s] us feel…that some structural situation we had become ready for…has jumped and become a different structural situation…" (175). In the present article, I do not presume to ascertain and judge what is an acceptable "figure of twins," and what is a "mere parading of synonyms." I believe we can better study and appreciate the development of de Vere's use of hendiadys by casting a wider net than does Wright. Doing so also allows us to see just how many word pairs de Vere coined and invented in this early work. Later writers paid tribute to many of them by borrowing them, in some cases dozens of times.

Wright observes that "Shakespeare's examples are dazzlingly various; the *developing* playwright appears to have taken this odd figure to his bosom and to have made it entirely his own" (169; emphasis added). We have a misleadingly limited picture and understanding of Shakespeare's development if we remain unaware of his earlier work, that has not yet been attributed to the same author.

Wright finds that Shakespeare's hendiadys "is always somewhat mysterious and elusive" (176). Wright speculates that "It may at times betoken [Shakespeare's] teeming mind" (173). At other times, he senses that it suggests "an oddly empty, discordant, and disconnected feeling…normal unions are disassembled" (175). Hendiadys "serves to remind us how uncertain and treacherous language…can be" (176) as it expresses "deceptive linking" (178). Wright is brilliant in perceiving the way de Vere increasingly used hendiadys to construct the extreme and enigmatic complexity of his writing— "hendiadys, far from explaining mysteries, establishes them…hendiadys resists logical analysis" (169), and it serves "at once to deny and to extend the adequacy of linguistic forms to convey our experience" (183). As Wright notes, the usual conjunction in hendiadys is "and," but in de Vere's use, it thwarts our expectation that we will be given a clear parallelism, which is "among our major instruments for ordering the world we live in" (169). Wright says Shakespeare's hendiadys can be "estranging" (173), and that it "usually elevates the discourse and blurs its logical lines, and this combination of grandeur and confusion is in keeping with the tragic or weighty action of the major plays" (171); "hendiadys is often characterized…by a kind of syntactical complexity that seems fathomable only by an intuitional understanding of the way words interweave their meanings" (171).

The psychoanalyst James Grotstein made a startingly similar observation about the way his own analyst Wilfred Bion made interpretations to him: he decided they were deliberately obscure, the better to evade his defenses, and thus speak directly to Grotstein's unconscious mind. So, here is another example of de Vere anticipating the discoveries of psychoanalysis by four centuries. Further, we might compare the verbal doubling of hendiadys with our binocular vision, which allows us to perceive the three-dimensional world in greater depth; so does hendiadys help us penetrate beneath the surface of language and its meanings, as our conscious mind is mesmerized by the shimmering tensions between the paired words. Cognitive psychology has expanded our understanding of memory, by distinguishing between two major memory systems—implicit and explicit. They have different neuroanatomical substrates. At one level, language activates the explicit, more conscious memory system. But good creative writers use words to evoke our less conscious and less verbal feelings, linked with implicit memory. De Vere was a master of this use of complex language to appeal to both parts of our minds. Hendiadys assisted him in doing so.

One of the several categories of hendiadys is the use of the second word to amplify the first. *Amplificatio* is a central rhetorical device, enacted in miniature form in hendiadys. The Psalms characteristically use repetition for intensification. They profoundly influenced de Vere, and probably contributed to his use of hendiadys for amplification and intensification. In addition, Wright discovers that Shakespeare sometimes uses the device for "an interweaving, indeed sometimes a muddling, of meanings, a deliberate violation of clear sense that is in perfect keeping with Shakespeare's exploration…of 'things supernatural and causeless'" (173).

One thinks of Richard II's extraordinary prison soliloquy, when he wonders how he can possibly compare his prison cell to the wide world, alone as he is. He famously concludes that "My brain I'll prove the female to my soul,/ My soul the father; and *these two* beget/ A generation of still breeding thoughts,/ And these same thoughts people this little world" (V.v.6-9; emphasis added). Four lines later, he says that the "better sort" of thoughts "do set the word itself/ Against the word" (V.v.13-14). Literally, the sometimes seemingly contradictory words of the Bible. More broadly, though, the generative potential of "word against word" reminds us of de Vere's continual use of the figure of hendiadys, throughout some forty years of his literary career. This generative genius of hendiadys forms close connections with the mind, and brain, of the reader and audience of de Vere's work, so that we ourselves become the "female" to de Vere's soul. It is known, for example, that listening to his poetry activates more parts of the brain than does listening to other poets. An ambiguous stimulus, whether a visual inkblot or its verbal equivalent, is most effective in drawing out unconscious contents of our own mind, which we project onto that uncertain prompt. De Vere is ever elusive and complex, and he seduces us into a collaborative partnership with his language, as we "hammer out" how we will people our minds with the still-breeding thoughts that de Vere engenders in us.

Wright is disappointed that Shakespeare scholars have shown so little interest in Shakespeare's style, especially "those stylistic devices that make for elusiveness…Hendiadys is too confusing, too disorderly…Critics…often take little interest in the figurative devices that seem merely decorative" (172). If these critics realized that "Shakespeare" also wrote the *Arte of English Poesie*, and translated *A Ritch Storehouse*, they would have more reason to re-examine Shakespeare's use of rhetoric.

Hendiadys is characteristic of the Latin poetry that had such a profound literary influence on de Vere. The 1570 translation is chock full of hendiadys, starting with its very title. "A Ritch *Storehouse or Treasurie*[116] for *Nobilitye and Gentlemen*" translates Sturm's title, "Ad Werteros Fratres, Nobilitas Literata." So, from the title on, de Vere doubles Sturm's more terse original, with de Vere's Mercutio-like effervescence and exuberance. Centuries before Hemingway and the restricting influence of his spare style, de Vere delighted in his expansive use of the English language. The dedicatory epistle is titled, "To the Right Honorable, vertuous, and my singuler good lord, Lord Philip Howard Erle of Surrey, all *felicitie and happiness*."[117] A third hendiadys, and we still have not gotten beyond titles (in both senses)!

The body of the dedicatory letter includes some seventeen further instances of hendiadys (six of them in the first sentence, and the other eleven in the letter's second and final sentence): "zeal and desire" [a commonplace] "service and duty" [5 earlier uses in EEBO], "more *excellent and precious* than *long or tedious*" [11 earlier uses], "infinite and exceeding" [one or two earlier uses], "reading and study" [8 earlier uses], "golden and honorable" [*unique use* until 1633], "noble and high" [9 earlier uses], "evil and unskillful" [*unique use*], "good and praiseworthy"[118] [*unique use* before 1600], "precious and goodly" [2 earlier uses], "pain and travail" [a commonplace, which occurs in the plural in de Vere's Ovid, line 910 of Book One], "pleasure and pastime" [a commonplace], "good and ample" [the *first* of 24 uses], "fruit and commodity" [a commonplace], "tedious or troublesome,"[119] and "rude and unfiled"[120] [the *first* of two uses in EEBO]. The last pair listed introduces a new meaning of "unfiled" as "not reduced or smoothed by filing; unpolished, *rude*," and does so twenty years before the first use of this meaning listed in the OED (in Spenser's *Faerie Queene*). De Vere may sometimes use hendiadys to suggest the meaning of his newly coined words.

Some of these pairs hint at a contrast between subjective and more objective states--"my *payne and traveyle* to be but *pleasure and pastime*." Subjective pain turns to pleasure; travail (which could mean a literary work at the time) turns to recreation, if and when the dedicatee finishes reading this work. I have quoted two examples of paired hendiadys, where the first and second words of the first pair contrast with the first and second words of the second pair, respectively.

"Evil and unskillful" is intriguing. At first glance, it seems to pair "wicked" with "inexpert," which jars a bit, especially in the context of the author's description of his own translation. But one OED definition of "evil," going back as early as 1530, is in fact "unskillful," in which case we would have exact synonyms. Here, there is ambiguity as to which meanings of "evil" are active. Just a few lines earlier, de Vere described the dedicatee as "vertuous," twice. "My evil…handling" also contrasts with the dedicatee's "good and praiseworthy desire," mentioned later in the same sentence. So this examples illlustrates the sort of disorienting complexity that Wright finds in Shakespearean hendiadys. Also intriguingly, de Vere's uncle Arthur Golding (or de Vere himself?) used the phrase "savage and unskillfull" in his 1565 translation of Caesar's *Martial Exploits in Gaul*, just five years before the present work.

De Vere's introductory "To the friendly reader" (which follows the dedicatory epistle) also overflows with hendiadys. The fourth sentence alone has five such word pairs: "But our time (alas) is so inclined, and as it were naturally bent to bestow upon *barren*[121] *and unhonest* fruites,[122] *precious and golden*[123] names, that neythere can *vertuous and prayseworthy*[124] workes enjoye their *due and deserved* [125]tytles, being *forestauled and defrauded* by the evill, neythere good deedes possesse their owne, and worthy termes being prevented by the meane."

Wright's subjective criteria might not deem all of these doublings to be true examples of hendiadys. On the other hand, Wright felt that more complex use of hendiadys grew over time out of Shakespeare's earlier "parading of synonyms." And we must remind ourselves that de Vere was about twenty years old when he translated the work at hand.

Naturally, the dedicatory letter was de Vere's own, not a translation from Sturm. But in comparing de Vere's translation of Sturm with that of Spitz and Tinsley, we can see de Vere's addition of hendiadys. There are several examples of word pairs on every page. For example, where the latter write simply "the *practice* of learned men," de Vere expands this to "the *use and custome* of the learned." Where our recent translators say of the Werter brothers that they have "a great *similarity* in *talent*," de Vere expands both nouns into "twins": "a great *agreement and similitude* in *disposition and wytte*." The former refer to the "*diligence* of your teacher"; de Vere, to "the *indevor and example* of your teacher." Where they say "a special *degree* of happiness," he writes "the chiefest *step and degree* of felicitie." They write "temperance in desires"; he puts it "*temperaunce and an honest measure* in delightes." Instead of "I shall prescribe," de Vere says "I wyll *appoynt and prescribe*." When they simply say "*bipartite*," de Vere writes "*bypartite and double*." Where they use "*collected*," de Vere writes "*gather and dispose*."

Later in the translation, there are countless more word pairs. Here, I omit the many examples that were commonplaces at the time. Instead, I focus on those that were first coined in *A Ritch Storehouse*. For example, the noun pair "use and practice" is the first of hundreds of uses in EEBO.[126] "Painful [i.e., painstaking] and industrious" is the first of 108 uses.[127] Significantly, the second use was in Angel Day's 1586 *The English Secretary*, dedicated to his employer, Edward de Vere.[128] "Store and varietie" is the first of 71 uses. "*Store* and choice," by the way, was the second of 15 uses. I mention it here because it was first used in the translation of Ovid's *Metamorphoses* that many of us attribute to de Vere himself. "Acceptable and welcome" is the first of 65 uses.

"Servile or slavish" is the first of 57;[129] "servile and slavish" was not used until 1572. "Slavish" suggests an intensification of "servile," as with the contrast between slave and servant. "Manners and inclinations" is the first of 53 uses;[130] it seems to suggest a contrast between learned "manners" and natural "inclinations." "Rules and bounds" is the first of 30. "Learned and politic" is the first of 23 uses,[131] including Robert Green in his 1592 *Repentance*. "Noble and commendable" is the first of 22 uses.[132] "Name and commendation,"[133] and "pawse [pause] or staye" are the first of 14 uses ["pause *and* stay" first appears in 1578]. "End and form" is the first of 13 uses.[134] "Art and language" is the first of 9. "Things and matter" is the first of nine uses; "using and handling" and "things and matter" the first of eight uses; "purpose and reason,"[135] "gardien [I assume "garden" was a misprint] or keeper," and "assay and attempt" are the first of six; "wisely and commendably,"[136] "adventures and travails [which also meant "travels"]," and "unapt and foolish"[137] are the first of four; "elocution or utterance,"[138] and "nature and comlinesse"[139] are the first of three; "*writing* and utterance," the first of two; as are "handling and *writing*," "comparing and applying" "addition and ablation," "devising and *writing*,"[140] "gather and dispose," and "letters and voyces." "Praiseworthy and earnest," "virtue and fealty [feudal fidelity toward one's lord],"[141] "endeavour and example," "abate nor faint," "gravity and fullness,"[142] "gravity and beautification," "oration or work," "comelinesse and delectation," "handle and polish," "plentiful and neat [elegant]," "bipartite and double," and "arte and similitude" do not appear elsewhere in EEBO. Significantly, most of these unique word pairs describes ideal rhetoric, inspiring de Vere's "inventio."

Earl Showerman has drawn attention to the influence of the Greek tragedians on de Vere. *A Ritch Storehouse* advises, "a maker of Tragidies [must] take Euripides, or Sophocles to be his pattern." In general, Sturm stresses the importance for any writer to emulate the good models of prior writers. This emphasis may have been one reason de Vere decided to "English" this very work—taking it as a model for a discussion of rhetoric.

In 1569 appeared a poem subscribed "A.G.," which I have also attributed to de Vere (see Chapter Two).[143] How does the pattern of hendiadys in that poem compare with *A Ritch Storehouse*, published merely a year later? It has a few examples, in the latter portion of the poem— "just and trew" [a commonplace]; "faithfulness and right" [unusual]; "great and long" [a commonplace]; and "weale and welfare" [first EEBO use is in 1600]. The first and third pair modify the word "accounts," as it is a commendatory poem on bookkeeping. De Vere's "Young Gentleman" poem includes "range and seeke" [the unique use recorded in EEBO until 1672]; and "carcke and care" [a commonplace].

In conclusion, I have presented evidence that Edward de Vere was probably the translator of the 1570 work, *A Ritch Storehouse or Treasurie for Nobilitie and Gentlemen*, written in Latin by Johann Sturm. It is an important precursor of de Vere's 1589 *Arte of English Poesie*. It shows the deep interest in rhetoric in general, and *inventio* in particular, that is also reflected in the works of Shake-speare. I devote special emphasis to the parallel fascination with the figure of hendiadys—"one through two"—that also characterizes the works of Shake-speare.

Chapter Four

A Wanderlust Poem, Newly Attributed to Edward de Vere[144]

> "A young Gentleman willing to travell into
> forreygne partes being intreated to staie in England:
> Wrote as followeth."
> from 1585 edition of *Paradise of Daintie Devises*

Who seekes the way to winne renowne,
Or flieth with winges of high desire
Who seekes to weare the Lawrell crowne,
Or hath the minde that would aspire,
Let him his native soyle eschewe
Let him goe range[145] and seeke anewe.

Eche hautie[146] heart is well contente,
With every chaunce that shall betide
No happe[147] can hinder his intent.
He steadfast standes though Fortune slide:
The Sunne saith he doth shine aswell
Abroad as earst[148] where I did dwell.

In chaunge of streames each fish can live,
Eache fowle content with every ayre:
The noble minde eache where can thrive,
And not be drownd in deepe dispayre.
Wherefore I iudge all landes alike
To hautie heartes that Fortune seeke.

To tosse the Seas some thinkes a toyle,
Some thinke it straunge abroad to rome,
Some thinke it griefe to leave their soyle
Their parentes, kinsfolkes, and their home.
Thinke so who list, I like it not,
I must abroad to trye my Lott.

Who lust at home at carte to drudge
And carcke and care[149] for worldly trashe[150] :
With buckled shooe let him goe trudge,
Instead of launce a whip to swash.
A minde thats base himselfe will showe,
A carrion sweete to feede a Crowe,

If *Iason* of that minde had binne,
Or[151] wandring Prince that came from *Greece*
The golden fleece had binne to winne,
And Pryams Troy had byn in blisse,
Though dead in deedes and clad in clay,
Their woorthie Fame will nere decay.

The worthies nyne[152] that weare[153] of mightes[154] ,
By travaile wanne immortal prayse:
If they had lived like Carpet knightes[155] ,
(Consuming ydely) all their dayes,
Their prayses had with them bene dead,
Where now abroad their Fame is spread.

This poem is unsigned. But it follows directly after three poems that have been attributed to de Vere. The first two are signed "E.O." ("If care or skill"; "The trickling tears"). The third poem ("I am not as I seem to be") is signed "E.O." in the 1576 first edition of the book; "E.Oxf." in the 1577 edition; and "E.Ox." in the 1585 edition. De Vere was the only *living* member of the nobility who allowed his name or initials to accompany some of his poems in this book. Why did he make these changes in his initials? It is easy to imagine that his peers at court criticized him for breaking with tradition and publishing poems subscribed with his initials. In view of de Vere's deeply defiant streak, I can further imagine that he expanded the "O." to "Oxf." and to "Ox." as a way of tweaking his critics-- like a rebellious adolescent who gets an additional body piercing each time her parents ground her. And we have the direct statement in *The Arte of English Poesie* that de Vere was "first" among the "Noble men... who have written excellent well as it would appear if their doings could be found out and made publicke with the rest" (p. 75).

The first two are in the same rhyme scheme as the present poem: six-line stanzas in ABABCC. The first two are in iambic pentameter, whereas this poem is in iambic tetrameter. Our poem is followed by "No joye comparable to a quiet minde," which is also iambic pentameter in the same ABABCC rhyme scheme); it may also be written by de Vere. The anonymous *The Arte of English Poesie*, which I have attributed to de Vere (see Chapters Six and Seven), especially recommends stanzas of six lines: "A staffe of sixe verses, is very pleasant to the eare" (p. 80).

There are eleven other unattributed poems in the 1585 edition; some or all of them may also be by de Vere. Ringler and May (2004) list all these poems as anonymous, with the exception of "Perhaps you think me bold," which they attribute to Arthur Bourdier. De Vere is the only author indicated by his initials, among the nine poets listed at the beginning of the book; it is possible that he agreed to have other poems published in this edition on condition of anonymity. Five anonymous poems in this edition are followed by the words "My lucke is losse" (after "FINIS," which ends each poem); this recurrent phrase may indicate common authorship. One such poem is "In Commendation of Musicke." Three lines from that poem are sung and discussed by musicians near the end of Act 4 of *Romeo and Juliet*. One of de Vere's poems that appears only the 1576 edition of *Paradise* ("Of the mightie power of Love") refers to Paris; "My lucke is losse" are the words spoken to Venus by Paris in George Peele's 1581 play "Arraignment of Paris."

Several factors lead me to attribute this poem to de Vere. Its placement directly after three poems signed with de Vere's initials is one clue. More significantly, its content closely matches the events of de Vere's life from 1574 to 1575 (when he was 24-25 years old). We know that de Vere asked Queen Elizabeth to allow him to travel to the Continent during both those years. She initially refused to give him permission for this trip. Headstrong as he was, he left for the Continent anyway. In July of 1574, he travelled to Flanders. The Queen was furious at his defiance, and she sent Thomas Bedingfield to retrieve him a few weeks later. A courtier wrote at the time, "I trust his little journey will make him love home the better hereafter. It were a great pity he should not go straight, there be so many good things in him to serve his God and Prince"

(Anderson, p. 71). An anonymous report on de Vere from August 7, 1574, states "The desire of travel is not yet quenched in [de Vere], though he dare not make any motion unto Her Majesty that he may with her favor accomplish the said desire" (Anderson, p. 72).

I assume this poem was written, then, in de Vere's effort to overcome the Queen's opposition to his desire to travel abroad. She relented and did allow him to spend more than a year on the Continent beginning in 1575. De Vere's poems in the first, 1576 edition of *Paradise* may have been written when he was 16 or younger (Richard Edwards, who compiled the 1576 edition, died in 1566). If de Vere is the author of "A Young Gentleman," it would be one of the few times we have strong clues about his age when he wrote one of his poems.

So much of the poem's content is consistent with what we know of de Vere's character. Even the word "intreated" in the title speaks volumes. The Queen gave commands-- she did not entreat[156] . But it was not the only time de Vere defied her orders. He later refused her repeated orders to dance for visiting Frenchmen in 1578 (Anderson, p. 142).

The Paradise of Daintie Devises went through seven editions from 1576 to 1600. Many poems were added and deleted through those several editions. For example, the 1577 edition omitted twelve poems from the first edition, and added ten new ones. There are two poems signed "E.O." in the 1576 edition that are deleted in all subsequent editions. A third "E.O." poem appears only in the 1576 through 1580 editions, and is deleted from subsequent editions. The unsigned poem, "He complaineth thus" follows two "E.O." poems in the 1576 edition and was subsequently deleted; it may be by de Vere.

We should note that *Paradise*, in its several editions, was a book of song lyrics. That is, every poem in the book was intended to be sung. De Vere's early signed poetry is thus in the form of song lyrics. And what do we know about Shakespeare as an author of song lyrics? Before the full impact of Looney's 1920 book first proposing that de Vere wrote Shakespeare, Shakespeare scholars emphasized Shakespeare's unique talent as a song writer—"One of the most attractive features in his lyrics is their spontaneous ease of expression. They seem to lilt into music of their own accord, as naturally as birds sing...*the author*, though primarily a dramatist, *could be among the greatest of song writers when he tried*" (Henry N. MacCracken, F.E. Pierce, and W.H. Durham, *An Introduction to Shakespeare*, New York: Macmillan, 1927 p. 71; emphasis added).

It is likely that Looney and previous editors of de Vere's poetry were using editions of the book that did not contain this poem, and they thus overlooked it. Why wasn't our poem included in the editions before 1585? We can only speculate. One surmise is that de Vere had to choose his battles with the Queen, since he repeatedly pushed her too far by his defiance. Publishing this poem any sooner might have rubbed her face in a public reminder of his unauthorized trip to Flanders, along with his other acts of insubordination. In the late summer of 1585, de Vere was sent to Holland on a military mission. Perhaps he decided his current favor with the Queen justified reminding her of his earlier trip. But he did not put his initials after this poem, suggesting a compromise between conflicting wishes to make it public, but avoid angering the Queen. It is instructive to notice and ponder such examples of de Vere playing with anonymity, moving back and forth across the line of identifying himself to his readers. It captures some of the social class aspects of anonymity for courtier poets, well before he tried to disguise his history plays as having been written by a commoner in order to optimize their propaganda value in enhancing commoners' loyalty to their Tudor monarch.

The poem was reprinted with many modifications in the second volume of J.O. Halliwell's 1841 *Early English Poetry*. It was re-titled, "In Praise of Seafaring Men." Halliwell unconvincingly attributes it to Sir Richard Greenville.

The imagery of the poem has three allusions to birds-- "flieth with winges of high desire" in the second line; "Eache fowle content with every ayre" in the third stanza; and "A carrion sweete to feede a Crowe" in the fifth stanza. Spurgeon, in her ground-breaking study of Shakespeare's imagery, singles out his use of birds as one of his most frequent tropes. Spurgeon observes that, with the exception of the human body, "Shakespeare's images from birds form by far the largest section drawn from any single class of objects" (p. 48). She further notes that it was the movements of birds that most interested him-- it is the flight of birds that he cited in the second line of this poem.   It is first the natural world that encourages the young gentleman to seek adventure abroad. It is the sun, then the fish, then the birds that stir his wanderlust. Spurgeon observes that it is nature in general that supplies the largest number of Shakespeare's images (p. 44).

Although many early modern poems dealt with travel, Ringler and May's first-line index of Elizabethan poetry lists this poem as the unique exemplar of their more specific category, "Travel--Defense of." Four additional poems are listed in the category of "Travel-- abroad, foreign."

The ambitiousness of the poet is strikingly clear. From the first line to the last, the poem speaks of an author who seeks to "winne renowne" and achieve widespread "Fame." The classical ideal of kleos aphthiton (undying honor) is evoked in references to "woorthie Fame [that] will nere decay" and in "immortal prayse." The poem constructs a dichotomy between two groups of men. The first group, like the poet, Greek heroes and the Nine Worthies, willingly face risks in order to win immortal fame; such a person has a "noble minde" that aspires. The second group have a mind that is base. They cautiously shirk the risks of travel. While avoiding the treacherous seas, they ironically drown in their own despair. They trudge in a *buckled* (crumpled) shoe and *swash* (bluster as with a weapon) their whip. These words in two consecutive lines evoke "swashbuckler," which meant a noisy braggadocio as early as 1556 (OED). They are homebodies who suffer indignities to play it safe, although ultimately they will be forgotten once their base lives end in humiliating death.

The phrase "drownd in deep dispayre" in the third stanza evokes the similar phrase "in deep distress are drowned" from de Vere's poem, "Loss of Good Name" ("Fram'd in the front of forlorn hope past all recovery..."). The phrase "my deepe dispayre" occurs twice in another unsigned poem of the 1585 edition, "Oppressed with Sorrow, He Wisheth Death." It also occurs in *Henry VI, Part 3* (as well as in many other early modern poems).

In a common play on the word, "travaile" in the final stanza alludes both to labor, and to the "travell" of the title. "Carpet knightes" in the final stanza refers to those who are content to remain safe at court or at home, shirking from the battlefield and thus never winning fame and reknowne. This is also the meaning of "carpet" in a line in *Twelfth Night* (III, iv, l. 258): "Knight... on carpet consideration." De Vere's uncle, Arthur Golding, used the phrase "carpet knights" in his 1564 translation of Justinus's *The Histories of Trogus Pompeius.*

Some other features of this poem are consistent with poetry of de Vere and of Shakespeare. Hendiadys (the expression of an idea by two words connected with 'and') is a frequent rhetorical device in Shakespeare, in de Vere's letters, and in two lines of "A Young Gentleman"-- "range and seeke" and "carcke and care." Shakespeare's sonnets recurrently deal with mortality, the passage of time, and the use of poetic creation to resist time's capacity to destroy what we value. The "renowne" that is sought the first line of "A Young Gentleman" becomes the "Fame that will nere decay" in the sixth stanza, and the "immortal prayse" of the seventh. "Abroad" appears for the third time in the poem's final line. Now, rather than describing where the young man yearns to go, it is means "everywhere." It is now used to describe the power of "Fame" to break free of the chains that limit mortals in time and space, giving to those who win high renown eternal and universal praise.

     The meter is strict iambic tetrameter. Alliteration and assonance abound. "Alike" and "seeke" are rhymed, as are "Greece" and "blisse." Of the fourteen words that begin the couplet lines, six (or 43%) begin with the letter "T." Shakespeare favored that initial letter in the couplets of his Sonnets-- 26% of those lines also begin with "T" words (as contrasted with roughly 15 % of the words throughout Shakespeare's works). Although many of de Vere's poems do not show such a pattern, another de Vere poem in *Paradise* ("His minde not quietly settled") has a third and final stanza of six lines, each of which begins with a "T" word (Thus, The, The, That, To, and That).

     In summary, I use converging lines of evidence to propose that "A Young Gentleman Willing to Travell" is a previously unattributed poem by Edward de Vere, author of the works of William Shakespeare. I would encourage others to explore the remaining unsigned poems in the various editions of *The Paradise of Daintie Devises* and research their possible authorship by de Vere.

REFERENCES

Anderson, Mark, *Shakespeare by Another Name: The Life of Edward de Vere, Earl of Oxford, the Man who was Shakespeare.* New York: Gotham Books. 2005.
Anonymous, *The Arte of Englishe Poesie.* Kent, Ohio: Kent State University Press. 1589/1970
Edwards, Richard, *A Paradise of Daintie Devises.* 1585. (STC 7520; on *EEBO*).
Nelson, Alan, *Monstrous Adversary: The Life of Edward de Vere, 17th Earl of Oxford.* Liverpool: Liverpool University Press.
Ringler, William A. and Steven M. May, *Elizabethan Poetry: A Bibliography and First-line Index of English Verse, 1559-1603.* New York: Thoemmes Continuum. 2004.
Spurgeon, Caroline, *Shakespeare's Imagery and What It Tells Us.* Cambridge: Cambridge University Press. 1935.

Chapter Five

A 1578 Poem about de Vere's Trip to Italy, entitled "A Letter written by a yonge gentilwoman and sent to her husband unawares (by a freend of hers) into Italy"

To my knowledge, this chapter is the first attempt to link this anonymous 1578 poem with Edward de Vere.[157] A detailed examination of the poem and its literary allusions suggests that it was written by de Vere. Definitive proof of this attribution must await the accumulation of further evidence. Even if de Vere was not its author, I maintain that it was written with him in mind.[158] Once that hypothesis is considered, possible connections with de Vere abound. It was published two years after he returned from his 14 months on the continent—most of that time having been spent in Italy.[159] The poem was published in Thomas Proctor's 1578 *Gorgious gallery, of gallant inventions Garnished and decked with divers dayntie devises, right delicate and delightfull, to recreate eche modest minde withall, first framed and fashioned in sundry forms by divers worthy workemen of late dayes.*

It was published two years after the first edition of *Paradise of Daintie Devises*, which contained several poems signed by de Vere. Its full title even repeats the phrase 'daintie devises' from that earlier title. The actual editorship of *Gorgious gallery* is somewhat obscure, as is that of *Paradise of Daintie Devises*. Hyder E. Rollins[160] speculates that Owen Roydon (whose 'address' and poem begin the book) was the original compiler of this collection, and that Thomas Proctor took it over after Roydon's death. Rollins calls Roydon an experienced compiler of miscellanies of poetry. But Rollins considers it strange that Proctor did not show much involvement in printing books. His career after 1584 was obscure.

The collection's original title was more provocative—*A Handful of Hidden Secrets*, which makes one think of the secret authorship of "A young gentilwoman." Many poems in the collection are anonymous; ten are signed with Proctor's initials. Several poems deal with separated lovers, and others are written—as is the present poem-- in the voice of a woman complaining of her false lover. They have an important literary precedent--Ovid's *Heroides*. It is a collection of 15 "complaint poems" in the voice of prominent women from classical mythology, including Dido, Medea, and Penelope. Those three, like the speaker in the present poem, have been abandoned by their lovers. Ovid believed he had created a new literary genre by writing these poems from the first-person perspective of their heroines. An English translation of the *Heroides* was published in 1567, and there was later something of a vogue for similar complaint poems in English, especially starting in the late 1580s. Ovid's genre was consistent with classical female lamentations. As scholar Barbara Newman writes of Greek literature, "a good woman was rarely seen and more rarely heard. One of the few speaking roles permitted her was lamentation."[161]

Anthony Munday, who worked as de Vere's secretary by 1579 and who, like Proctor, was an apprentice of John Allde, wrote commendatory verses for *A Gorgious Gallery*.[162] Matthew Steggle, in his ODNB article on Proctor, writes of the book that it "had a complicated gestation," and that, "to modern readers, its most interesting individual item is 'The History of Pyramus and Thisbie Truly Translated,' a translation which may possibly have given Shakespeare material for *A Midsummer Night's Dream*."

There is a recurrent pattern of obscure authorship and editorship in Elizabethan anthologies of verse. The many editions of Tottel's *Miscellany* were not all accurately dated. Richard Edwards was dead for ten years when the first of many editions of his *Paradise* was published. The first edition of *Hundreth Sundrie Flowres* was anonymous; there was then a radically different 2d edition, now attributed to Gascoigne. The present poem contains three phrases that had only been used once before (according to *EEBO*'s[163] current data) in *Hundreth Sundrie Flowres*: "thou hast thy will"; "furious fate"; and "wretched dame."

There was no second edition of *Gorgious Gallery*. According to Rollins, it was only after many years that a second copy of the formerly unique early edition was found. Rollins maintains that the book had little influence on Elizabethan writers. Only Thomas Nashe and Thomas Dekker mentioned it. This is consistent with the speculation that the book was suppressed once de Vere reconciled with his wife Anne, and evidence of their past estrangement was censored.

De Vere's separation from Anne after his return from Italy publicized his doubts that he was the father of her child, born while he was abroad.[164] Although Anne was pregnant when de Vere left for the Continent, he seemed certain he was not the father. In the poem, the speaker refers to her paternally abandoned child as the circumstance "that greeves mee most." As is well known, de Vere refused to live with Anne for several years after he returned from the Continent in April of 1576. De Vere wrote a furious letter to Lord Burghley one week after he returned to England from the Continent. He was enraged that his father-in-law was meddling in de Vere's relationship with his wife Anne. De Vere expresses his intense displeasure to Burghley that his personal affairs "had not needed to have been the fable of the world if you would have had the patience to have understood me" (Anderson, p. 117). Anderson maintains that "De Vere would spend the rest of his life writing about the dramatic and traumatic events of his twenty-sixth year" (p. 118).

The present poem appears to be an early case in point. Lord Burghley, his father-in-law, wrote to Queen Elizabeth on April 23 of that year, asking her to intercede to persuade de Vere to reconcile with Anne and to limit the public scandal of his claim that her child was illegitimate. One might speculate that the Queen insisted that de Vere consider Anne's position. This poem might then have been part of de Vere's response, showing his capacity to imagine Anne's feelings of betrayal that began while he was in Italy, and exploded when he shunned her upon his return.

It would be in character for de Vere to turn to his literary genius when he had something important to say to Queen Elizabeth, in view of their mutual love of poetry. I have previously speculated that de Vere petitioned the Queen for permission to visit the Continent through a poem.[165] In fact, several words and phrases in the 1578 poem echo that very poem. I have also speculated that his petition for the thousand pound annuity the Queen eventually granted him was the first draft of *The Arte of English Poesie*[166], much of which is addressed to her in the second person.

The author of *The Arte* draws attention to the pivotal role played by the highly developed imagination of the poet—"(if it be not disordered) [it is] a representer of the best, most comely, and beautiful images or appearances of things to the soul and according to their very truth. If otherwise [i.e., if the imagination becomes "disordered" or impaired], then doth it breed chimeras and monsters in man's imaginations, and not only in his imaginations, but also in all his ordinary actions and life which ensues" (p. 110).[167] If he wrote these words-- which I believe he did-- de Vere may have been recalling his years of "disordered" jealousy of Anne, and the devastating effect his monstrous jealousy had on Anne's life. The same phenomenally creative imagination that produced the best works of literature in history could also plague de Vere with unbearably obsessive jealousy. By contrast, in his chapter on "The form of poetical lamentations," the author of *The Arte* perceptively observes that the poetic expression of grief about the "torments of love" (cf. the present poem) can be cathartic—"Lamenting is altogether contrary to rejoicing... and yet is it a piece of joy to be able to lament with ease and freely to pour forth a man's inward sorrows and the griefs wherewith his mind is surcharged...making the very grief itself (in part) cure of the disease" (p. 135).

Could someone other than de Vere have written this poem? Perhaps. Although I strongly suspect de Vere was its author, I cannot establish his authorship definitively. What about the fact that the speaker in the poem is a woman? If we take this authorial voice literally, as proof of the poet's actual identity, de Vere's wife Anne must be considered. When I first encountered this poem, I did consider the possibility she wrote it. In turn, this reminded me of the poems attributed to Anne on the death of her infant son in 1583-- poems that are now assumed to have been written by John Soowthern.[168] That is, I wondered if the present poem was similarly ghost-written for Anne. However, one argument against Anne having written or commissioned the poem is the unlikelihood she would have allowed such a poem to be made public. She did not seem to share her husband's penchant for notoriety. Further, many aspects of the poem suggest de Vere's authorship.

For example, some words and phrases in the poem are consistent with de Vere's writing, including his pattern of coining words. One word in the 1578 poem ("surpassed" as an adjective) is the earliest such use listed in *EEBO*, much earlier than the first instance cited in the *OED*. Among my glosses on the poem are evidence of possible Shakespearean literary allusions—both by this poem, and also to this poem.[169] Some phrases are the first (or only) usage cited in *EEBO*. Other phrases were earlier used by writers connected in various ways with de Vere—Brooke, Gascoigne, Golding, Lyly, and Munday. For example, "Thou hast thy will" occurs in this poem, as it does in Shakespeare's Sonnet 135 and in his *3 Henry VI*. We know de Vere was especially inventive in his use of language. He seemed to have a photographic memory for what he read, so that certain phrases in this poem may reflect conscious or unconscious literary allusions on his part.

I assume *A young Gentleman willing to travell into forreygne partes, being intreated to staie in England: Wrote as followeth* (YGM) was circulating in manuscript by 1578, so that readers of this *Yonge Gentilwoman* would detect the intertextuality between them. Let me highlight a few of these parallels. Both rhyme "soyle" with "toyle"; both rhyme "win" with "bin" [been]. The present poem asks "doost though love to gad abroad"; YGM states "I must abroad." The present poem has "the golden Fleese is wonne"; YGM says "The golden fleece had binne to winne."

As a playwright, de Vere showed an extraordinary capacity to step into the shoes of another person, and speak convincingly from their subjective point of view. If de Vere was putting himself in Anne's position during this poem, it suggests that he did not believe she had any real understanding of the powerful feelings that drew him to Italy. Both poems seem to refer to de Vere's 14-month trip to the Continent in 1575-76. The present poem has "Eneas," whereas YGM spoke of Troy, the original city of Aeneas. Hyder E. Rollins notes that Dido and Aeneas was a favorite topic in Elizabethan ballads (154).

Mark Anderson,[170] among others, speculates that the 1577 court play *A Historie of Error* (a precursor of *The Comedy of Errors*) was written by de Vere, and that in it he makes "self-deprecating jokes at his own jealous rage" (p. x) and "pathological behavior" (p. 125) toward his wife Anne. De Vere's unusual "negative capability" included his rare flair for seeing himself as others saw (and sometimes ridiculed) him. If he exploited that capacity in writing his plays, it is plausible to speculate he put himself in his wife's shoes in this poem, as though he is writing her character in an autobiographical play.[171] Thus, I do not believe we are required to take the female voice in this poem as literally proving its author was a woman.

Many Oxfordian commentators view de Vere's guilt over his mistreatment of Anne to be a central dynamic in his psychology, that blossomed into his brilliant treatment of pathological jealousy in several of his plays. The present poem may thus give us a window into the nascent process of de Vere stepping outside his jealous rage and narcissistic mortification, instead looking at things from Anne's point of view. He does so brilliantly and poignantly in this poem. Although we do not know with certainty just when this poem was written, we can assume it was written between 1576 and 1578. A couple of years later, de Vere wrote his "Echo Poem" in the voice of his lover Anne Vavasour. Thus, we have another example of de Vere writing a poem from the perspective of a woman in his life.[172]

Caroline Spurgeon immeasurably enriches our understanding of Shakespeare through her close reading of his characteristic choices of imagery. Spurgeon observes that the largest group of images in Shakespeare concerns nature (e.g., the "tiger"); of these, "by far the greatest number is devoted to ...the gardener's point of view" (pp. 45-46; cf. the "tender sprig"). The "guideless ship" and "the seas are calmer to return" in this poem recall Spurgeon's further conclusion that "the next largest section [of Shakespeare's nature imagery] is the sea, ships and seafaring" (p. 47). One of the largest categories of images found in Shakespeare by Spurgeon is mythological (in this poem, Jason and Medea; Aeneas and Dido; Bacchus's priestess; and Jove). Further, Spurgeon notes that in *All's Well That Ends Well*, Helena speaks of the astrological influence of the stars under which a person was born. Helena (a character similar to de Vere's wife) speaks variously of a "charitable star" (I.i.185); "baser stars" (I.i.191); and "luckiest stars" (I.iii.250). The last contrasts with the "luckless star" of the 1578 poem.

Examining earlier and later uses of words and phrases from this poem is illuminating. Let me give an especially interesting example. One line of the poem entreats the narrator's husband to return quickly—to "retire with speed." The earliest use of that phrase in *EEBO* is in Willliam Thomas's 1549 *The historie of Italie* (London: Thomas Berthelet). It refers there to the retreat of King Charles VIII of France, after invading Italy in 1494. The context tells a story that may have provided de Vere with some of the plot and character names of *The Tempest*. Lodovico Sforza encouraged this French invasion, in order to get Charles's help in becoming the Duke of Milan. King Alfonso II of Naples opposed Sforza, who had usurped the rightful place of Alfonso's son-in-law as Duke of Milan.

As Charles's invasion headed toward Naples, Alfonso abdicated his throne in favor of his son *Ferdinand*. Alfonso then spent the rest of his life on the island of Sicily, in a monastery. One could say that he, like Prospero, was driven to that island by the treachery of the usurping Duke of Milan. As Thomas puts it, he there "disposed himself to studie, solitarinesse, and religion." In *The Tempest*, Prospero is Duke of Milan, but gives administrative authority to his brother Antonio, so he will have more time to devote to his books. Antonio then usurps power, and exiles Prospero, who lands on an island where he devotes his time to solitary study and magic (cf. "religion"). In the play, it is Alonso (no "f") who is King of Naples, and *Ferdinand* is his son. It is likely that de Vere identified with Alfonso, especially as he neared the end of his own life.[173]

In summary, identifying a poem Edward de Vere may have written—a poem that transparently addresses a crucial episode of his life-- enlarges our understanding of his temperament and of his creativity. It also helps us reconstruct a bit of de Vere's poetic work between the early poems signed "EO" and his later work signed with his famous pseudonym. I have used multiple, converging lines of evidence to build the case that de Vere was the author of this anonymous 1578 poem. I have shown that its content fits nearly precisely with a well-documented crisis in his life, when his wife Anne gave birth to their first child while he was living on the Continent. I believe that this is a work of considerable poetic skill. It seems to deliberately echo an earlier poem de Vere wrote about his desire to travel to the Continent. A large number of its phrases are found in the works of Shakespeare. Other phrases echo those in important literary sources of de Vere. It shows de Vere's capacity for empathy with the internal experience of his antagonist. The speaker of the poem counters her husband's groundless jealousy with protestations of her "loyalty" and her innocence of "life unchast."

"A Letter written by a yonge gentilwoman and sent to her husband unawares[174] (by a freend of hers) into Italy"[175]

Imagine[176] when these blurred lines, thus scribled[177] out of frame[178],
Shall come before thy careles[179] eyes, for thée to read the same:
To bee[180] through no default of pen, or els through prowd[181] disdayne,[182]

But only through surpassing greefe,[183] which did the
Author payne.

Whose quivring hand could have no stay, this carful[184] bil[185]
to write
Through flushing teares[186] distilling fast, whilst shee did it
indite[187]:
Which teares perhaps may have some force (if thou no
tigre bée[188]),
And mollifie thy stony hart[189], to have remorse[190] on mée.

Ah perjurde[191] wight reclaime[192] thy selfe, and save thy
loving mate,[193]
Whom thou hast left beclogged[194] now, in most unhappy
state[195]:
 (Ay mee poore wench) what luckles star[196]? what
frowning god[197] above?
What hellish hag[198]? what furious fate[199] hath changd our
former love?

Are wée debard our wonted joyes? shall wée no more
embrace?
Wilt thou my deare in country strang, ensue[200] *Eneas* race:
Italians send my lover home, hée is no *Germayne* borne,[201]
Unles ye welcome him because hée leaves mée thus
forlorne.

As earst ye did *Anchises* sonne,[202] the founder of your
soyle,
Who falsely fled from Carthage Quéene, reléever of his
toyle:[203]
Oh send him to *Bryttannia* Coastes, unto his trusty féere,[204]
That shee may view his cumly corps,[205] whom shée
estemes so deere:

Where wee may once againe renue, our late surpassed[206] dayes,
Which then were spent with kisses sweet, & other wanton playes:[207]
But all in vayne (forgive thy thrall,[208] if shee do judge awrong),
Thou canst not want of dainty Trulles[209] *Italian* Dames among.

This only now I speake by gesse, but if it happen true,
Suppose that thou hast seene the sword, that mee thy Lover slue:
Perchance through time so merrily with dallying[210] damsels spent,
Thou standst in doubt & wilte enquire from whom these lines were sent:

If so, remember first of all, if thou hast any spowse,
Remember when, to whom and why, thou earst hast plited vowes,
Remember who esteemes thee best, and who bewayles thy flight,
Minde her to whom for loyalty thou falshood doost requight.

Remember Heaven, forget not Hell, and way thyne owne estate,
Revoke[211] to minde whom thou hast left, in shamefull blame & hate:[212]
Yea minde[213] her well who did submit, into thine onely powre,
Both hart and life, and therwithall, a ritch and wealthy dowre:[214]

And last of all which greeves mee most, that I was so
begylde,
Remember, most forgetfull man, thy pretty tatling[215]
childe:
The least of these surnamed[216] things, I hope may well
suffise,
To shew to thee the wretched Dame[217], that did this bill
devise.

I speake in vayne, thou hast thy will,[218] and now sayth
Aesons sonne,[219]
Medea may packe up her pypes,[220] the golden Fleese is
wonne:[221]
If so, be sure *Medea* I will, shew forth my selfe in deede,[222]
Yet gods defend[223] though death I taste, I should distroy
thy seede:

Agayne, if that I should enquire, wherfore thou doost
sojurne,
No answere fitly mayst thou make, I know, to serve thy
turne:[224]
Thou canst not say but that I have, observ'd my love to
thée,
Thou canst not say but that I have, of life unchast bin frée.[225]

Thou canst not cloak (through want) thy flight, since riches
did abound:
Thou néedes not shame of mée thy spouse, whose byrth
not low is found,
As for my beauty, thou thy self, earwhile didst it
commend,
And to conclude I know no thing, wherin I dyd offend:

Retier[226] with speed, I long to see, thy barke in wished bay,
The Seas are calmer to returne, then earst to fly away:
Beholde the gentill windes doo serve, so that a frendly gayle[227],
Would soone convay to happy Porte[228], thy most desired sayle:

Return would make amends for all, and bannish former wronge,
Oh that I had for to entice, a *Scyrens*[229] flattering songe:
But out alas, I have no shift,[230] or cunning to entreat,
It may suffise in absence thine, that I my griefes repeate.

Demaund not how I did disgest,[231] at first thy sodayne flight,
For ten dayes space I tooke no rest, by day nor yet by night:
But like to *Baccus* beldame Nonne,[232] I sent and rangde apace,
To sée if that I mought thée finde, in some frequented place:

Now here, now there, now up, now down, my fancy so was fed,[233]
Untill at length I knew of troth, that thou from mee wert fled:
Then was I fully bent[234] with blade, to stab my vexed harte,
Yet hope that thou wouldst come agayn, my purpose did convart:[235]

And so ere since I liv'd in hope bemixt with dreadful feare,
My smeared[236] face through endles teares[237], unpleasant doth appeare:

My slepes unsound with ugly dreams[238], my meats are
vayn[239] of taste
My gorgious rayment is dispilde[240], my tresses rudly
plaste.

And to bee breefe: I bouldly speake, there doth remayne no
care:
But that therof in amplest wise, I doo possesse a share:
Lyke as the tender sprig[241] doth bend, with every blast of
winde,
Or as the guidelesse Ship on Seas, no certaine Porte[242] may
finde.

So I now subjecte unto hope, now thrall to carefull dread,
Amids the Rocks, tween hope and feare, as fancy mooves,
am led:
Alas returne, my deare returne, returne and take thy rest,
God graunt my wordes may haue the force, to penytrat thy
brest.[243]

What doost thou thinke in *Italy*, some great exployt to
win?[244]
No, no, it is not *Italy*, as sometimes it hath bin:[245]
Or doost thou love to gad[246] abroad,[247] the forrain costes[248]
to vew,
If so, thou hadst not doone amisse, to bid mée first adew:

But what hath bin the cause, I néede not descant[249] longe,
For sure I am, meane while poore wench, I only suffer
wrong:
Wel thus I leave, yet more could say: but least thou
shouldst refuse,
Through tediousnesse to réede my lines, the rest I will
excuse:

144

Untill such time as mighty *Jove* doth send such luckye grace,
As wée therof in fréendly wise, may reason face to face.[250]
Till then farwell, and hée[251] thee kéepe, who only knowes my smart:[252]
And with this bill I send to thee, a trusty Lovers harte.

By mee, to thee, not mine,[253] but thine,
Since Love doth move the same,
Thy mate, though late, doth wright, her light,
Thou well, canst tell, her name.[254]

Chapter Six

A Shakespearean Snail Poem, Newly Attributed to Edward de Vere[255]

"In prayse of the Snayle"
from *Paradise of Daintie Devises* (from 1585 on)

The deepe turmoyled[256] wight[257], that lives devoyde of ease,
Whose wayward[258] wittes are often found, more wavering[259] then the seas:
Seekes sweete repose[260] abroad[261], and takes delight to rome,
Where reason leaves the Snayle for rule[262], to keepe a quiet home.

Leape not before thou looke, lest harme thy hope assayle,
Hast havocke makes in hurtfull wise, wherfore be slow as S[n]ayle[263]:
Refrayne from rash attempt, let take heede be thy skill[264],
Let wisedome bridle[265] brainsicke[266] wit[267], and leasure[268] worke thy will[269].

Dame reason[270] biddes I say, in thynges of doubt be slacke[271],
Lest rashnesse purchase[272] us the wrong, that wisedome
wills us lacke:
By rashnesse divers[273] have bene deadly overcome,
By kindly[274] creepyng on like Snayle, duke *Fabe*[275] his
fame hath wonne.

Though some as swift as hawkes, can stoope[276] to every
stale[277],
Yet I refuse such sodayne[278] flight, and will seeme slow as
Snayle:
Wherefore my prety[279] Snaile, be still and lappe[280] thee
warme,
Save[281] envies[282] frets[283] mauger[284] their fumes[285], there
few shall do thee harm[286].

Because in some respect, thou holdes me to be wise,
I place thee for a Precedent, and signe before mine eyes:
Was never any yet, that harme in thee could find,
Or dare avow that ever Snaile, wrought[287] hurt to humaine
kinde.

I know dame Phisicke doth, thy friendly helpe implore,
And crav's the salve from thee ensues[288], to cure the crased[289]
sore[290]:
Sith Phisicke then avowes, the vertues in degree[291],
In spight of spight[292] I weare thee still[293], that well
contenteth me.

Caroline Spurgeon, in her marvelous, path-breaking book on Shakespeare's use of imagery, singles out the unusual range of Shakespeare's sympathy, which extends not only to humans, but to a wide variety of animals. She observes that most of us think of the snail primarily as being slow, so that comparisons of a person to a snail are derogatory. She argues that Shakespeare was primarily impressed by the snail's emotional sensitivity. She supports her thesis with quotations from two plays and from a long poem.

"The snail seems to him an example of one of the most delicately sensitive organisms in nature; it is "love's feeling" only that "is more soft and sensible/ Than are the tender horns of cockled snails" (*Loves Labors Lost* IV,3,336). In *Venus and Adonis* (l. 1033), he writes of the feelings of the "snail, whose tender horns being hit,/ Shrinks backward in his shelly cave with pain,/ And there all smother'd up in shade doth sit,/ Long after fearing to creep forth again." Spurgeon asks us to "Notice how he emphasises the greater poignancy of mental than physical pain, even in a snail." And in Coriolanus, Aufidius "Thrusts forth his horns again into the world;/ Which were inshell'd when Marcius stood for Rome,/ And durst not once peep out" (p.107).

Even when he is citing the snail's proverbial slowness, Shakespeare does so sympathetically, as in the schoolboy "creeping like snail/ Unwillingly to school" (*As You Like It*, II.vii). Barker (1996) expands on Spurgeon's study of the snail in two of Shakespeare's plays and in other early modern dramas. She argues that snail imagery in that period is "indicative of fundamental cultural anxieties," and is "an image of decay of demarcation in general." Spurgeon notes that the snail would not be the most obvious candidate for a poet's sympathy. She might have added that Elizabethans were still influenced by the medieval notion of the Great Chain of Being, with God on the highest level, the oyster on the bottom of both the ocean and the animal branch of this Chain, and the snail closer to the oyster than to Man. But our poet begins by calling the snail a "wight," which immediately implies a kinship with humans, since "wight" can refer both to people and to animals.

Spurgeon's example of Shakespeare's unusual sympathy with the snail supports the attribution of "In prayse of the Snayle" to de Vere, author of Shakespeare's works. Whoever the poet was, he was very much a kindred spirit of Shakespeare's. As with her three examples, the poet finds many virtues in the snail. Even its slowness is portrayed as a virtue, in contrast with the hazards of hastiness. The anonymous author of *The Arte of English Poesie* (probably de Vere) cites Emperor Augustus's motto, *festina lento*, or "make haste slowly." The poet's snail exemplifies this advice.

In 1580, Gabriel Harvey ridiculed some of the clothing fashions that de Vere brought back with him from Italy. In particular, he compared his cap to an oyster. It is possible that de Vere identifies with the snail in this poem partly as a defiant retort to Harvey's taunt.

The Shakespearean works that Spurgeon cites for sympathetic images of the snail are relatively early ones. Londré speculates that the first draft of *Loves Labours Lost* was written by de Vere in 1577. That may have been close to the time our poem was composed. *Venus and Adonis* was probably written in 1592.

Our poem has a misleading simplicity, if we stop at its surface. What could be simpler than a harmless snail? Yet more disturbing allusions abound. In particular, many words in the poem allude to mental disturbances of various sorts. Thus far, I have glossed only one set of meanings of several words in the poem. Examining the poem a bit more closely, we see that the hapless snail keeps veering toward the precipice of mental instability. "Turmoyled" can mean tormented and thrown into confusion. "Wayward wittes" can allude to loss of one's reason, as does the reference to reason leaving and no longer ruling. "Brainsicke" can refer to madness. "Frets" can mean an agitated state of mind, "fumes" can be something that clouds one's reason, and "crased" can mean crazed or insane.

As in the typical Elizabethan court masque, the dangers outlined in the first two stanzas threaten chaos, until the day is saved by Dame Reason, Duke Fabe, and Dame Phisicke. Another transition occurs midway through the poem—starting with "Wherefore my pretty Snaile" in the fourth verse, the remainder of the poem is an apostrophe to the snail.

The fifth stanza is brimming with Biblical[294] phrasing. We know how much the Bible influenced Shakespeare, and how consistent de Vere's Biblical annotations are with Shakespeare's works (see Stritmatter). "I place thee for a..." recalls four Biblical instances of "I... give thee for a..." and one "I set thee for a..." "Before mine eyes" alludes to five Biblical uses of the phrase "before mine," all but one of them being exactly this phrase, "before mine *eyes*." The word "signe" occurs 73 times in the Geneva Bible. Eight of those times, or more than 10 per cent, are in Ezekiel, a book that was heavily annotated by de Vere. It usually alludes to a message from God as a "signe of the covenant," a phrase found three times in Genesis.   In fact, the fifth stanza can be read as having been spoken by God.

In the third chapter of Exodus, Moses hears the voice of God speaking to him from the burning bush. After being told to demand that Pharaoh release the Jews, Moses asks God a series of questions. In his reply, God said, "And this is the sign for you that I Myself have sent you" (Alter, p. 320; Exodus 3:12). Alter's commentary acknowledges the ambiguity of just what this sign is. It may be God's voice speaking from the burning bush. Two verses later, God answers Moses's question about his name with his famous "I AM THAT I AM" (capitalized in de Vere's Bible). That phrase famously appears in de Vere's 1584 letter to Burghley, and in Sonnet 121.[295]

A "signe" also alludes to a divine miracle, or a way of keeping God's commandments. "I will place thee for a Precedent" alludes strongly to Isaiah 49:6, "I wil also give thee for a light of the Gentiles," and to Jeremiah 6:27, "I have set thee for a defence and fortresse among my people."

"Wrought hurt" uses the Biblical past tense of the verb "to work." Many of the 88 uses of the word in the Geneva Bible are pejorative—what is wrought is villenie, abomination, wickedness, evil, follie, and treason. "Snayle" occurs once in the Geneva Bible, and twice in the Bishop's Bible. Psalm 58:8 states "Let him [the wicked man] consume like a snaile that melteth, and like the untimelie frute of a woman, that hath not sene the sunne" in the former[296], and "Let them creepe away lyke a snayle that foorthwith consumeth to naught" in the latter. The snail was thought to melt away both because of the track of slime it left behind, and also because snails would sometimes perish on hot rocks in the desert. It is also striking that this unique use of "snail" in the Geneva Bible was just before a reference to a woman having a miscarriage or stillbirth ("like the untimelie frute of a woman"), possibly as divine punishment[297]. (The Bishop's Bible also include the snail in a list of "uncleane thynges that creape upon the Earth" [Leviticus 11:30].)

The second stanza contains several proverbial phrases. "Thy hope" from its first line is a phrase that occurs only once in the Geneva Bible, in the book of Proverbs, in the consoling statement, "For surely there is an ende, and thy hope shall not be cut off" (Proverbs 23:18). "Thy will," the last two words of the second stanza, allude to the Lord's Prayer. All but one of the times that phrase is used in the Bible are in reference to doing God's will.

These many Biblical echoes alert us to a theological dimension of the entire poem. Like some of the Sonnets, the entire poem reads like a secular version of some Christian hymn of praise, starting with its title. The poulter's measure used in the poem is still used to the present day for some Christian hymns (where it is now called "short meter"). All the poems in *The Paradise of Daintie Devices* were lyrics, meant to be sung.

Read allegorically, the first line, "The deepe turmoyled wight, that lives devoyde of ease," sounds like a reference to post-Edenic man. The "thynges of doubt" of the third stanza may allude to spiritual doubt. There is an implicit contrast between religious faith and "Dame reason." The "creepyng" wight in the final line of the third stanza makes the reader think not just of the snail, but of the Edenic snake. The descent of the hawk in the next line may thus allude to the fall of Man that resulted from succumbing to the serpent's temptation. "I place thee for a ... signe before mine eyes" in the fifth stanza may then evoke Numbers 21:9—"So Moses made a serpent of brasse, and set it up for a signe, that as many as are bitten may looked upon it, and live." This is the only Old Testament reference to a sign that was cited by Jesus. In John 3:14-15, Jesus compares himself to that bronze serpent. In the Bible, bronze is a metal connected with God's judgment. The fifth stanza ends with an implicit contrast between the Edenic snake and the harmless snail, who never "wrought hurt to humaine kinde."

The eight times "signe" is used in Genesis and Exodus are all passages where the speaker is God. A passage in 2 Chronicles (32:24) points to the poem's final stanza, in alluding to a sign from God which consoles a sick person: "In those days Hezekiah was sicke unto death, and prayed unto the Lorde, who spake unto him and gave him a signe."

I suspect de Vere enjoyed the contrast between "brainsicke" and "Phisicke"—the latter word enacts an undoing of the state of being sick. The mucus that the snail secretes is called the "salve" that offers "helpe" and "cure" to those who suffer "craséd sores."[298] To the early Christians, the snail was a symbol for the resurrection, and for the immortality of the soul. Jesus was a healer who offered mankind the "salve" of salvation (cf. "salve me," Latin for "save me"). The medicinal properties of snail slime were known to Galen and Hippocrates. Pliny recommended it for burns and skin infections, since it has antibiotic effects. He also advocated snails for fits of madness. In de Vere's day, one author recommended it as an ingredient in a treatment of fever, and of "felon" (a sore on the finger) ("T.C." *An Hospitall for the Diseased*, 1578). Bullein (1579) claimed that "Snayles cleneth the iyen [eyes], helpeth the Eares, and is wholsome for bone ache" (p. 81). Some skin creams sold today contain snail mucus, and recently the Food and Drug Administration has shown interest in possible medicinal uses of snails.

I find it likely that de Vere wrote this poem in response to a specific challenge that he faced in his life. It reads as a defense of his chosen course of behavior, in response to real or imagined criticism that he was being too slow in taking some proposed action. De Vere certainly needed the advice he offers in this poem—his life was filled with rash, headstrong, impulsive, self-destructive actions. As I argued in an earlier article (Waugaman, 2007), de Vere was the only living member of the nobility who allowed his initials to be subscribed to some of the poems in *Paradise of Daintie Devices*. This fact alone increases the likelihood that some of the anonymous poems in the book were also written by him. If "In praise of the Snayle" is in fact by de Vere, its anonymity suggests the poem alludes to circumstances that were too sensitive for de Vere's authorship to be made public. I suspect the reference to hawks that are caught in a net when they follow a lure is a key to the events in de Vere's life that inspired this poem. He may have written it after he returned from the Continent, and refused to become ensnared in married life with Anne, despite the entreaties of Lord Burghley to act quickly in acknowledging his paternity of her infant daughter. He cannot be accused of impetuosity in waiting three years before he resumed living with his wife.

He alluded to Burghley's pressure to act quickly one week after he returned to England in a letter to him-- "Urged... by your letters to satisfy you the sooner..." He rebukes Burghley for the latter's lack of "patience," and he announces, "I mean not to weary my life anymore with such troubles... nor will I, to please Your Lordship only, *discontent* myself" (Anderson, pp. 116-117; my emphasis; cf. "that well contenteth me," the poems final words).

If his estrangement from his wife occasioned this poem, it would highlight another set of meanings in it. Snails were long thought to be associated with femininity and with fertility. Some species are hermaphroditic. Ancient medicinal uses of the snail included several uses in the treatment of pregnant women. Pliny believed snails could help speed childbirth. Galen advised snails for hydrops fetalis[299]. And de Vere's estrangement from his wife was precipitated by his accusation that another man had impregnated her. "Thynges of doubt" might thus allude to doubts about who was the father of his wife's child.

The historical record shows that his wife sought an abortion for that pregnancy from the Queen's physician, Richard Master (Anderson, p. 118-119). De Vere learned his father-in-law, Lord Burghley, was failing to keep their agreement to allow de Vere to live apart from de Vere's wife—Burghley planned to ask the Queen to intervene to pressure de Vere to end his marital estrangement. On July 13, 1576, de Vere wrote Burghley, warning him to drop that plan. His letter includes the statement, "For always I have and will still *prefer mine own contentment* before others…" (Anderson, p. 121; emphasis added). The final words of our poem, "that well contenteth me," may echo the sentiment of that letter, as well as his earlier refusal to "discontent myself."

Most of Shakespeare's sonnets have various connections with other contiguous or distantly placed sonnets. Similarly, this poem has several echoes of another anonymous poem of the 1585 and later editions—"A young Gentelman willing to travell into forreygne partes."[300] In particular, the first stanza of the present poem shares *nine* key words with the other poem, occurring in six of the latter poem's seven stanzas (deepe, live[s], seas, seekes, sweete, abroad, rome, leave[s], and home). The closely similar "lives" and "leaves" of the first stanza imply that one must leave home in order to live, just as "live" and "leave" have the same implication in the other poem. The first four lines thus seem to constitute a sort of subliminal summary of the other poem, while simultaneously introducing a fresh topic. No other stanza includes nearly as many words that are shared with the other poem. I assume both poems reflect his intense conflicts about his successive homes and his relatives who reside in them. I believe both poems were inspired by his trip to the Continent.

The poem's rhyme scheme is that of rhymed couplets throughout. The first stanza rhymes "rome" and "home,"[301] offering an early contrast between those two alternatives, which are reconciled by the snail, who takes his home with him. In the third stanza, "overcome" and "wonne" are imperfect rhymes to the ear, though they are closer rhymes to the eye, since "m" and "nn" look so similar. The poem's meter is iambic, with six feet alternating with seven feet. This so-called "poulter's measure" was popular with Elizabethan poets. Saintsbury calls it "a sort of bridge and compromise between literary and popular verse" (p. 311). Its alternating length, shorter then longer, echoes the iambic structure of each foot. There is a caesura midway through each line of hexameter, and after the fourth foot of each line of heptameter. Steven May (1980), an authority on de Vere's poetry, calls him "a competent and fairly experimental poet" who used eleven different metrical and stanzaic forms (including poulter's measure) in the sixteen poems that May definitely attributes to him.

In summary, I have presented several arguments for attributing the 1585 poem "In praise of the snayle" to de Vere.

REFERENCES

Anderson, Mark, *Shakespeare by Another Name: The Life of Edward de Vere, Earl of Oxford, the Man who was Shakespeare.* New York: Gotham Books. 2005.
Anonymous, *The Arte of Englishe Poesie.* Kent, Ohio: Kent State University Press. 1589/1970.

Barker, Jill (1995). "Wooed by a snail: Testaceous Androgyny in English Renaissance Drama." *Imprimatur* 1: 20-30.

Bullein, William (1562). *Bullwark of Defence against all Sicknes, Sornes, and Woundes.* London: Thomas Marshe

Edwards, Richard, *A Paradise of Daintie Devises.* 1585. (STC 7520; on *EEBO*).

May, Steven (1980). *Studies in Philology* 77:1-132.

Rollins, Hyder Edward (1927). *The Paradise of Dainty Devices* (1576-1606). Cambridge, MA: Harvard University Press.

Stritmatter, Roger (2001). *The Marginalia of Edward de Vere's Bible: Providential Discovery, Literary Reasoning, and Historical Consequence.* Northampton, MA: Oxenford Press.

Saintsbury, George (1923). *A History of English Prosody.* 2d edition. Vol. I. London: Macmillan.

Spurgeon, Caroline (1935). *Shakespeare's Imagery and What It Tells Us.* Cambridge: Cambridge University Press.

"T.C." (1578). *An Hospitall for the Diseased*, London: R. Tottell

Waugaman, Richard M. (2007). "A Wanderlust Poem, Newly Attributed to Edward de Vere." *Shakespeare Matters.*

Chapter Seven

A Ribald Ignoto Poem[302]

J. Thomas Looney, who was the first to propose de Vere wrote Shakespeare's works, also recognized that 'Ignoto' was another of de Vere's pen names.[303] It seems likely that de Vere borrowed that pseudonym from the Latin Vulgate translation of Acts 17:23. This verse contains St. Paul's description of coming across an altar "unto the unknown god" in Athens. Here's the verse in the Geneva translation: "For as I passed by, & behelde your devocions, I founde an altar wherein was written, UNTO THE UNKNOWN GOD, Whome ye then ignorantly worship, him shewe I unto you." In Latin, "unknown god" is "Ignoto deo."

So de Vere is identifying himself with that unknown god-- rebranded by St. Paul as the Judeo-Christian God-- in his pseudonym Ignoto. There is the additional hint that de Vere hoped, in choosing "Ignoto" as a pen name, that he too-- like the "unknown god"-- would one day be correctly identified by some latter-day St. Paul, such as Looney himself.

But there is more. I had noticed that Acts 17:28 (that is, five verses below the one I just quoted) reads "For in him we live, and move, and have our being, as also certeine of your own Poetes have said, For we are also his generacion." A Genevan marginal note offers this gloss on "Poetes"-- "As Aratus and others." The italicized phrase is the fifth line of the poem "Phaenomena," by Aratus. This illustrates, by the way, the quality of the scholarship of the Geneva Bible printed marginal notes. (Aratus was a popular Greek poet of the third century BCE.)

Is it common for secular poets to be quoted in the New Testament? I posed that question to Professor Bart Ehrman, a leading New Testament scholar at the University of North Carolina at Chapel Hill. He said Acts 17:28 is the only such instance of which he is aware. Another significant aspect of Acts 17:28 is that it is the only occurrence of the word "Poet/s" in the Geneva Bible. This may be yet another reason that de Vere, fond as he was of his Geneva Bible, decided to borrow Ignoto as one of his pen names.

"I love thee not for sacred chastitie": A 1599 Anonymous Poem I attribute to de Vere

IGNOTO.

I Love thee not for sacred chastitie,
who loves for that? nor for thy sprightly wit:
I love thee not for thy sweete modestie,
Which makes thee in perfections throane to sit.

I love thee not for thy inchaunting eye,
Thy beauties ravishing perfection:
I love thee not for unchast luxurie,
Nor for thy bodies faire proportion.

I love thee not for that my soule doth daunce,
And leap with pleasure when those lips of thine:
give Musicall and gracefull[304] utterance,
To some (by thee made happie) poets line.

I love thee not for voice or slender small,
But wilt thou know wherefore-faire sweet for all.

Faith (wench) I cannot court thy sprightly eyes,
with the base Viall placed betweene my Thighes:
I cannot lispe, nor to some Fiddle sing,
Nor run uppon a high strecht Minikin.

I cannot whine in puling Elegies,
Intombing Cupid with sad obsequies.

I am not fashioned for these amorous times,
To court thy beutie with lascivious rimes.
I cannot dally, caper, daunce and sing,
Oyling my saint with supple sonneting.
I cannot crosse my armes, or sigh ay me,
Ay me Forlorne egregious Fopperie.
I cannot busse thy fill, play with thy hayre,
Swearing by love, Thou art most debonaire.
Not I by Cock, but shall tel thee roundly,
Harke in thine eare, zounds I can (   ) thee soundly.

Sweet wench I love thee, yet I wil not sue,
Or shew my love as muskie Courtiers doe:
Ile not carowie a health to honor thee,
In this same bezling drunken curtesie.
And when als quafde, eate up my bowsing glasse,
In glory that I am thy servile asse.
Nor wil I weare a rotten burbon locke,
As some sworne pesant to a female smock.
Wel featurde lasse, Thou knowest I love the deere:
Yet for thy sake I wil not bore mine eare,
To hang thy durtie silken shootires there.
Nor for thy love wil I once gnash a brick,
Or some pied collours in my bonnet stiche.
But by the chaps of hell to do thee good,
Ile freely spend my Thrise decocted bloud.

If Looney was correct in speculating that "Ignoto" was one of Edward de Vere's pseudonyms, was this poem the work of de Vere? To my knowledge, it is the only surviving poem in which "Ignoto" appears above the poem, rather than beneath it, as a subscription. The reason for this placement is obscure. I believe that de Vere may have composed this poem. If so, it deserves to be better known and studied.

Like Sonnet 130 ("My mistress' eyes are nothing like the sun"), this poem lampoons the "false compare" of a conventional tribute to one's lady. In so doing, it satirizes current courtier fashions. Smitten courtiers are expected to "groan" (Sonnet 130, lines 6 and 10; Sonnet 133, line 1), but the poet "cannot whine in puling Elegies." The poem's first section repeats six times, "I love thee not for--." The fifth line is "I love thee not for thy inchaunting eye," recalling the first lines of two Dark Lady sonnets: "Thine eyes I love, and they, as pitying me" (Sonnet 132) and "In faith, I do not love thee with mine eyes" (Sonnet 141). Having negated a series of conventional praises of one's love, the poet announces in lines 21-22, "I am not fashioned for these amorous times,/ To court thy beutie with lascivious rimes," explicitly rejecting the "fopperie" of current courtly fashion.

Why "thy bodies faire proportion"? Wouldn't "bodies fair shape" have been just as suitable? In addition to metrical needs, "proportion" has further a meaning which is activated by the next stanza, when it explicitly introduces the theme of music. Only then would the early modern reader realize "proportion" means not just "shape," but also "musical rhythm and harmony." That next stanza refers to the lips of the "sweet wench" musically reading or singing a line of poetry. "Proportion" alludes not just to shape or musicality, though. A few lines later, the poet puns bawdily on "base Viall" as both a bass viol and the semen container—both located between his thighs. This trope of a musical instrument to refer to a bodily part reflects yet another implication of "thy bodies faire proportion"—the wench's body as an instrument the poet will play.

The final section skewers "muskie Courtiers" as drunken louts. Line 33 seems to coin the verb "carowie" based on "carrow" as gambler who exploits the titled and wealthy with "drunken curtesie." The poet decisively rejects being such a fawning "servile ass." Having rejected the model of courtiers as inebriated sycophants, the poet next rejects the effeminacy of courtly convention. He will not tie a ribbon around a long lock of his hair and wear it in front of his shoulder in the womanly style of a portrait of the adolescent Earl of Southampton. I believe line 38 coins "smock" as a verb meaning "to render effeminate," a few years before the OED gives 1614 as the first instance of this meaning. If this is correct, "to a female smock" means "turned into a female." If "smock" is a noun, "female" would be redundant, since it meant a female undergarment.

The third section replies to the first section's repeated "I love thee not for--." Line 31 begins the section with the first declaration of "I love thee." This is repeated in line 39, "Thou knowest I love the deare." But it then continues to ridicule courtier fashions, as the poet says he will not "bore" his ear. This means not only to pierce one's ear. It alludes to a biblical verse that stipulates that piercing a hole in a person's ear signifies that they are a slave (Exodus 21:6). So the poet is refusing to be "thy proud heart's slave and vassal wretch" (Sonnet 141, line 12).

The poet adds the insulting criticism that his lass's shoe ribbons are "durtie." He closes with further ribaldry. Having ended the second section with the claim that he will [expletive deleted] her soundly, he ends the poem with "Ile freely spend my Thrise decocted bloud." In addition to the echo of "Cock" from line 29, the "third decoction" refers to the contemporary theory of physiology, whereby blood was thought to be transformed into a secretion such as sweat, tears, or—in this case—semen.

Chapter Eight

The Arte of English Poesie: The Case for Edward de Vere's Authorship[305]

      Whigham and Rebhorn's (2007) edition of *The Arte of English Poesie* provides us with a much needed opportunity to re-examine the authorship of this important, anonymous work of 1589. The *Arte* is widely recognized as possibly the most important Elizabethan book on literary theory. It is directed at courtiers, advising them not only on writing poetry, but also on proper behavior and dress. Whigham and Rebhorn accept the conventional theory that George Puttenham (1529-1591) was the book's author. They underline the book's central emphasis on the art of deception. Yet they fail to take the next step and consider the possibility that the book's author has successfully practiced this art of deception on the readers of his book over the ensuing centuries. I will argue that we do *not* in fact know with certainty who wrote this classic, and I will suggest that the author was Edward de Vere (1550-1604), who deliberately disguised his authorship of this book by planting false clues that scholars have accepted at face value. I hope to show that de Vere's claim to authorship is more compelling as that of Puttenham, the traditional author.

In making this case, I expect to encounter the usual entrenched resistances to relinquishing traditional authorship attributions. One major intellectual discovery of the early modern period was inductive reasoning, which starts with a clean slate, and develops theories based on empirical evidence. Ironically, when it comes to authorship attributions studies, we often regress to Aristotelian logic, that begins with an unquestioned premise, and reasons deductively from that initial premise. This gives the weight of tradition undue authority, and results in an irrational prejudice that traditional attributions must be accepted unless there is overwhelming evidence to the contrary. Scholars are often unaware that they then filter out evidence that contradicts traditional beliefs before they have weighed that evidence objectively. The bar for minimal evidence is set higher for subsequent authorship attributions than it is set for establishing initial attributions. The burden of proof is always on those—such as Oxfordians—who attempt to replace the traditional author with an alternative. We must realize that the result of this reasoning is that while it may protect us from false new attributions, it also leads to the rejection of valid new attributions. The only way to avoid such cognitive distortions is to begin with a clean slate, and evaluate evidence for the traditional candidate (e.g., Shakespeare of Stratford; or Puttenham) with the same stringency to which we subject evidence for competing candidates.

Willcock and Walker, in their 1936 edition of the *Arte*, acknowledged that "it is impossible to establish George Puttenham's claim to the authorship of the *Arte* with any finality" (xxxi). Steven May, in the *Oxford Dictionary of National Biography* [ODNB], concluded that Puttenham's claim to authorship is "not indisputable," but that it "trumps that of any other candidate." May's strongest evidence is Harington's 1590 reference to the book's author as "Putnam," and Bolton's 1610 reference to "Puttenham" as the author (these claims will be explored below). May saw evidence of Puttenham's rhetorical skills in a 1571 legal case. Puttenham's inventory of his ninety books shows that he owned books on law, rhetoric, French history, politics, and Latin poetry. May felt that, since John Throckmorton was involved with Puttenham's affairs and is praised in the *Arte*, this is further suggestive evidence of Puttenham's authorship.

Despite the disclaimers of Willcock, Walker, and May, most scholars now treat Puttenham's authorship as definitively established. So it is important to underline its weaknesses. In acknowledging some of these weaknesses, May admits that "George Puttenham the fugitive excommunicant is not easily reconciled with Puttenham the author." May further states that Puttenham's translation of a fragment of Suetonius "bears faint witness to his literary interests"; his library inventory omits any reference to English poetry 'such as... Tottel... or the works of George Gascoigne and George Turberville, all drawn on heavily in the *Arte*, and all in print by 1576, the date of Puttenham's inventory. The author claimed to have studied at Oxford and to have been brought up in foreign courts. As May admits, *neither* was true of George Puttenham (nor of his brother Richard, a weaker claimant to authorship). Yet scholars still treat other autobiographical material in the *Arte* as though it must be taken at face value, and that it therefore invalidates de Vere's authorship.

When the *Arte* was discussed in a seminar devoted to it at the 2009 Shakespeare Association of America, Whigham, Rebhorn, and May each acknowledged that there are many unanswered questions about the book.[306] May noted, for example, that early modern publishers made their profit on subsequent editions of books, since first printings were typically too small to recoup all their expenses. But the *Arte* was never re-printed after its first edition. With its many woodcuts, May said it would have been an expensive book to print, and its publication may have been subsidized. May's recent archival research failed to make a convincing case for Puttenham's authorship.

The Stronger Case for de Vere's Authorship

The *Arte* was published anonymously, and most previous commentators have not speculated as to why Puttenham never claimed authorship of this well-regarded book. The legend that Puttenham wrote it started with John Harington's 1590 written request to the *Arte*'s printer, Richard Field, that he publish Harington's forthcoming book "in the same printe that Putnams book ys." This feeble straw is the foundation on which the attribution of the *Arte* to Puttenham has been built. Ironically, Harington himself subsequently offered much stronger evidence that the author was actually one "Ignoto"; I will show that this pseudonym in every instance probably alluded to de Vere, and that Harington knew this.

In 1610, Edmund Bolton, in *Hypercritica*, reported a rumor that "one Puttenham, gentleman pensioner to Queen Elizabeth, wrote the *Arte*." However, May continues, "Neither George nor [his brother] Richard served as pensioners or in any other capacity under Elizabeth." May then concludes, unpersuasively, "yet clearly [sic] someone named Puttenham wrote the *Arte*." I would contend that May exemplifies Marcy North's central thesis that scholars abhor an authorship vacuum, and that he thus fails to give adequate weight to the possibility that authorship of the *Arte* has never yet been conclusively established.

I suggest that it is more parsimonious to conclude instead that, by 1610, there were two mutually incompatible rumors about the identity of the author, both of which may have been false. It is possible that Edward de Vere himself helped spread the deliberate disinformation that "Putnam" wrote the book.[307] This possibility is consistent with de Vere concealing his later work behind Shaksper of Stratford, as well as his possibly concealing his commentary on Edmund Spenser's *The Shephearde's Calender* behind Spenser's friend Edmund Kirke ("E.K.") in 1579. There may well be[308] a partial truth contained in the 1610 rumor-- I believe the *Arte* did have everything to do with a royal pension. It is likely that some insiders knew this origin of the *Arte*. They would have known that de Vere was successful in winning the royal pension he sought, in 1586, three years before the *Arte*"s publication.[309]

My hypothesis is that de Vere wrote an earlier draft of this book as a document addressed to the Queen alone, with the goal of obtaining the unprecedented 1,000 pound annuity that she granted him in June, 1586.[310] He justified his petition with the *Arte*'s list of past monarchs who had rewarded their favorite poets.[311] He told the story of Alexander the Great sleeping with a copy of Homer under his pillow. In fact, that passage uses a phrase that re-appears in the works of Shakespeare. The *Arte* states that the poems of Homer "were laid under his pillow and by day were carried in *the rich jewel coffer of Darius*." The highlighted phrase also occurs in *Henry VI, Part 1,* 1,5,25, as Charles is praising Joan of Arc—"In memory of her when she is dead,/ Her ashes, in an urn more precious/ Than *the rich-jewell'd coffer of Darius*."

172

Another example—"King Henry VIII, her Majesty's father, for a few psalms of David turned into English meter by [Thomas] Sternhold, made him groom of his privy chamber, and gave him many other good gifts" (107). This metrical translation of the Psalms, finished by other poets, is bound at the end of de Vere's Geneva Bible. Using the 20 psalms de Vere annotated (usually with ornate manicules, or pointing hands), I have found a wealth of previously unnoticed but pivotal literary sources for the works of Shakespeare.[312] The Sonnets, *The Rape of Lucrece, Titus Andronicus*, and the history plays are especially rich in newly discovered echoes of the marked metrical psalms.[313] The *Arte* also lists Sternhold first as one of the premier poets under King Edward VI; again, this respect is consistent with de Vere echoing the Sternhold psalms so pervasively.

It is likely that the Queen liked de Vere's draft so much that she encouraged him to expand and publish it, in order to foster the flowering of English poetry that marked her reign. If this hypothesis is correct, it is an important instance of de Vere's anonymous publication as early as 1589. Two poems published anonymously in the 1585 *Paradise of Daintie Devises*[314] have been attributed to de Vere.[315] De Vere apparently wrote one of these poems in an eventually successful attempt to win the Queen's permission to travel to the Continent. This hypothesis would establish an important precedent for de Vere's using his literary skill to win the Queen's favor. Chapter 19 of Book One of the *Arte* may have been de Vere's eloquent brief pleading for the Queen's commission for his writing the pro-Tudor "Shakespeare" history plays. The chapter champions the persuasive power of "poesy historical," while emphasizing that it is all the more instructive if it is not slavishly factual. It cites Xenophon as a "well-trained courtier" who wrote a "feigned and untrue" history of a monarch, that was beneficial for posterity (and, importantly, beneficial for the monarch's future image).

The exuberant tone of the *Arte*, while taxing one early reader[316], is consistent with de Vere's personality, as well as his role as leader of the euphuist movement. A central feature of the book is that it is written to the Queen. It is *not* dedicated to her (in fact, it is dedicated to Lord Burghley, de Vere's father-in-law and former guardian), but it is repeatedly *addressed* to her in the second person. These facts are consistent with my speculation about the circumstances of its composition.

The book evinces an irrepressible impulsivity of expression, including in its (Shakespearean) bawdiness. For example, the author teases the reader with the (im)propriety of his explanation of the etymology of epithalamion. ("Here, if I shall say that which appertaineth to the art and disclose the mystery of the whole matter, I must and do with all humble reverence bespeak pardon of the chaste and honorable ears, lest I should either offend them with licentious speech, or leave them ignorant of the ancient guise in old times used at weddings, in my simple opinion nothing reprovable... the tunes of the songs were very loud and shrill, to the intent there might be no noise out of the bedchamber by the screaking and outcry of the young damsel feeling the first forces of her stiff and rigorous young man" [139].) The author even praises the Queen's breasts and nipples (implying he had seen them).[317] A contemporary, while attesting to de Vere's position as one of the Queen's favorites in 1571, when he was 21 years old, wrote, "If it were not for his fickle head, he would surpass all of them [other courtiers] shortly" (*Dictionary of National Biography* [DNB]). The DNB entry also notes that his "perverse humour" was a source of "grave embarrassment" for Lord Burghley.

Whigham and Rebhorn perceive many traits in the author of the *Arte* that are consistent with de Vere's character. They note the centrality of deception and disguise in the book. Even figures of speech are defined as deceptions. Further, "By aggressively calling attention to the courtier-poet's duplicity, Puttenham creates a moral problem for him [the courtier-poet] (and for himself)" (55). De Vere's exile from court in the early 1580's is consistent with their observation that "Puttenham's authorial address... bespeaks his complex but abiding sense of disenfranchisement" (56). The sharp ambivalence with which they characterize the author's attitude toward court is consistent with de Vere's likely bitterness about his recent public humiliation by the Queen. Whigham and Rebhorn note "the author's own (partial and leaky) self-dissembling" (56)—their observation is consistent with my attribution to de Vere.

The Stratfordian Marcy North (2003) persuasively documents the prevalence of anonymous authorship in early modern England.[318] She (1999) (inadvertently) provides powerful arguments that support de Vere's authorship of the *Arte*. She convincingly highlights the central importance of literary anonymity in the *Arte*, in the context of "a society that delighted in *hidden names*" (p. 2, emphasis added). She steers us away from any simplistic interpretation of the role of anonymous authorship in the Elizabethan period. She instead finds "perpetual changes, continuous tensions... between the dangers and benefits of making one's name public" (9). I will examine North's arguments in light of de Vere's possible authorship of the *Arte*.

If de Vere wrote under pseudonyms, the *Arte*'s exploration of anonymity may be crucial in assessing de Vere's possible authorship of Shakespeare's works. The Elizabethans' use of anonymity made it "an evocative but surprisingly indefinable convention" (4), "a silent request for acknowledgement within a circle of insiders" (5). North elucidates the many subtle implications it had. For the courtier, literary anonymity offered a chance to enact Castiglione's ideal of *sprezzatura*, or "non-chalance" about receiving credit for one's poetic creations.[319] The goal was often to be well-known enough as a poet that insiders would correctly identify the courtier's anonymous poems, even though outsiders would not. North shows compellingly that the author of the *Arte*, by remaining anonymous, added further layers of complexity to the contradictory advice he gave to the reader about literary anonymity.

North shows that concealment is a central theme in the *Arte*. Its advice about proper courtly conduct only *seems* explicit-- she demonstrates that there is another level of "mystification" of "intricate social codes" beneath the surface. Referring to the author's anagram on Queen Elizabeth's name,[320] she says the author "suggests that identity functions like natural talent. Even when disguised or altered, an important name will shine through the veil to call attention to itself. Puttenham's anagrams verge on the supernatural," in that the author implies divine providence helped him create his anagram (10). North concludes that the message is that "The noblest form of identity announces itself without the aid of a patron or friend... Puttenham's name games ...demonstrate how poets might have hoped their identities would emanate from their work even when their names were not attached" (10-11).

North's thesis about the importance of deception in the *Arte*, and in Elizabethan society, is greatly strengthened by Arthur M. Melzer's *Philosophy Between the Lines: The Lost History of Esoteric Writing*,[321] about our blind spot for hidden meanings in the writings of past centuries. The severe political and religious restrictions, as well as the strict censorship of books in the Elizabethan era, make it likely that writers wrote on different levels, for the general public versus for insiders. A public name versus a secret actual name of the author is fully consistent with that pattern.

There is a story about a man who reacted with great humility to any recognition he received. A friend rebuked him acerbically-- "You're not important enough to be humble." Similarly, only courtiers who were "important enough" could succeed with the ploy of anonymous authorship. North writes of anonymity's "double-edged function as concealer and revealer, its potential to lead to fame or to obscurity," and she links this with "the *Arte*'s ambiguous depiction of anonymity as a mark of social status, one that paradoxically must be visible in order to be effective" (2). She feels certain that the anonymous author takes pleasure from the intricacies of the revelation of concealed names. He "works by the assumption that devices which alter or conceal a name say more about the historical person, not less... The disguising of the name points to an identity which is potentially more revealing than a proper name" (13).

North missed crucial opportunities to draw further plausible conclusions about the author of the *Arte*. She is artfully ambiguous in her only explicit reference to the authorship of this book-- "an author, *now thought to be* George Puttenham" (3; emphasis added).[322] Her tentativeness is a fitting acknowledgement that this commonly accepted attribution has never been definitively established. North's entire argument would be immeasurably enriched by the tantalizing possibility that de Vere has successfully concealed his authorship of this book until the present day.

North believes that the author expressed "dismay that social protocol could persuade talented gentlemen to suppress their works and their names in order to retain the respect of the court" (5). She then quotes the well-known line about "many notable Gentlemen in the Court that have written commendably, and suppressed it agayne, or els suffred it to be publisht without their owne names" (5). A similar passage in the *Arte* lists de Vere as the *first* example of such Gentlemen.[323] Consider the further layers of complexity and irony if de Vere is here commenting on his own anonymous works, including the *Arte* itself. It suggests that de Vere was saying for the record that he was publishing this book anonymously under duress.

North does not pursue some further implications raised by the *Arte*'s anonymity. The book's inconclusive attribution to Puttenham rests partly on shaky internal evidence, and partly on rumors during the decades after the book's publication. As we speculate about the book's authorship, we are playing the very game the author describes, trying to establish ourselves as the insiders who can penetrate the author's disguise and successfully identify him. Previous scholars have often regarded the author's clues about his identity as reliable ones, left deliberately, or through carelessness. They seem to overlook the possibility that the author was serious about disguising his identity.[324] For examples, many scholars now falsely assume that Puttenham was also the author of an *anonymous* collection of seventeen poems called the "Parthenaides" that claimed to be a New Year's gift for Queen Elizabeth. These poems were not published until 1811. Attributing them to Puttenham betrays circular reasoning—there is absolutely no independent evidence for such an attribution. The author of the *Arte* has dragged some red herrings across his trail, and these have thrown scholars off his scent. In so doing, he put into practice some of the complex attitudes toward anonymity that North so perceptively describes.

How do we know *what* the author of the *Arte* was thinking in publishing his book anonymously? We usually put ourselves in the other person's shoes, and imagine why we might have acted as they did. Such implicit identifications are often helpful. But the anonymous author serves as a Rorschach card, whose ambiguity inevitably elicits projections of our own psychology. So we must be mindful of the cultural context the author lived in. We now live in the age of plagiarism, which departs radically from former conventions of literary anonymity.[325] A frequent underlying premise in literary studies of anonymity is that the author had a predominant wish to be identified. This belief projects what North identifies as *our* abhorrence of the vacuum of anonymity. This may mislead us into a false assumption that the anonymous author surely provided us with reliable clues because she must have wanted us to unlock the mystery of her identity.[326]

Was there in fact a "stigma of print" in the early modern period? May (1981) shows that some noblemen did publish poetry under their own names in this period. But North cites with agreement J.W. Saunders' evidence in favor of such a stigma. And North names de Vere as one of the Elizabethan poets whose attributed work is so scarce because of "the courtiers' fashion of limiting readership through close manuscript circulation" (8). She next notes that "Whether poems are extant or common today is hardly an accurate measure of their effectiveness in early court circles" (8). This conclusion is consistent with the high esteem in which de Vere's contemporaries held his poetry, plays and interludes,[327] despite the paucity of the former and the absence of the latter in what has survived under his name.

If de Vere's contemporaries knew of his authorship, would they not have identified him in the historical record? North addresses this question indirectly in speculating that some Elizabethan compilers of anonymous poetry, such as John Lilliat, knew the identity of an anonymous poet, but chose to respect that anonymity rather than violate it.

North finds it "paradoxical" that the author *names* poets such as de Vere who wrote anonymously, but she adds that "it conforms to the principle that a reader's revelation of the author is seemlier than self-naming" and it "completes a cycle of concealment and revelation" (7). "Paradoxical" is something of an understatement when we consider the possibility that de Vere himself wrote the *Arte*. The alternating layers of concealment and revelation are then like Russian dolls, challenging the reader's certainty, and constantly keeping him or her off balance. This is consistent with Shakespeare's genius for creating and maintaining tension among various interpretations of motivation and meaning in his words, characters, and plots.

The *Arte*'s inventiveness in introducing new words rivals Shakespeare's. In fact, it was the *Arte* that coined the verb "coin" as meaning to create a new word. The *Arte* alone is the source of some 1,164 examples of word usage in the OED, compared with 1,370 for the complete works of Marlowe, 4,848 for Jonson, and 6,554 for Shakespeare. The OED lists 179 of these words as used for the first time in the *Arte*. Naturally, some were used earlier, but have not survived in print. For example, the OED and EEBO give the *Arte* as the first work to use "wedspite" and "spitewed," but the *Arte* itself attributes these coinages to Sir Thomas Smith, who happened to be de Vere's tutor. One cannot help but think of de Vere's "spite" that he married his guardian's daughter, Anne Cecil.

The *Arte* may well include more such examples than any other single early modern book. Many of the coined words in the *Arte* are English versions of Greek and Latin terms of rhetoric and of poetics, only some of which have endured. These include anaphoric, dactylic, and trochaic. Many more words that were coined in the *Arte have* endured in general usage. Such words include anagram; baiting; beaked; climax; colon [as a punctuation mark]; dramatic; emphasis; encomium; exemplary; exigence; grandiloquence; harmonically; impertinency; indecency; installment; major-domo; marching; and misbecoming.

Many of the coined words echo Shakespeare's language. Crystal noted that Shakespeare coined 309 words beginning with "un." According to the OED and EEBO, the *Arte* coined unfloor, unleave [to strip of leaves], and unveritable. And de Vere's surviving letters include what seem to be early uses of unacquaint, underage, and unsettled.

An especially salient example of a coined word is "hendiadys." De Vere coined this English word in the *Arte*, from the equivalent Greek word. He called it "the Figure of Twins," giving as an example "with venom and with darts," instead of simply saying "with venomous darts" (261-262). And the book itself is chock-full of hendiadys. We have already seen that de Vere's transations of Ovid's *Metamorphoses* and Sturm's *Ritch Storehouse* reflected his Shakespearean use of frequent word pairs. We find the same pattern in the *Arte*. A single sentence in Book One, Chapter Three newly coins *four* examples of hendiadys: "And Orpheus assembled the wild beasts to come in herds to hearken to his music and by that means made them tame, implying thereby how by his *discreet and wholesome* lessons uttered in harmony and with melodious instruments, he brought the rude and savage people to a more *civil and orderly* life, nothing, as it seemeth, more *prevailing or fit* to *redress and edify* the cruel and sturdy courage of man than it" (96). De Vere was a noted musician and may have felt inspired by the example of Orpheus to outdo himself in the rhetorical invention of profuse, "harmonious" hendiadys in this sentence. Book Three, Chapter One, begins with a sentence containing nine examples of hendiadys, five of them introduced here for the first time in EEBO.

Willis (2003) draws many connections between the *Arte* and the works of Shakespeare. Although I do not share his belief that Puttenham was the author of both, I agree with him that one person did in fact write both. That hypothesis finds a range of support in the pages of the *Arte*. We read, for example, of someone (Philino) who hid "behind an arras cloth" (218), reminiscent of the location where Polonius was killed by Hamlet. The *Arte* shows an intimate knowledge of stage-craft. It praises dramatists. Edward Ferrers is described as having "much more skill and magnificence in this meter, and therefore wrote for the most part [for] the stage in tragedy and sometimes in comedy" (148). In another passage, we read of "Firteus the Poet being also a *lame* man & *halting*" (108); in Sonnet 89, de Vere writes, "Speak of my *lameness*, and I will straight *halt*." De Vere's months is Italy is consistent with at least four passages where the author of the *Arte* writes of having been there. E.g., "being in Italie conversant with a certain gentleman…" (180); "I my selfe having seene the Courts of France, Spaine, Italie…" (356).

Caroline Spurgeon (1935) used an intriguing methodology to understand the mind of Shakespeare, by discerning what specific types of imagery occurred to him as he was writing his works—his typical patterns of visual association, as it were. Borrowing her assumptions, we can approach some details of the *Arte* in a similar way. For example, what number came to mind when the *Arte*'s author wanted to speak of the many rules that govern English poetry? *"[T]wenty other curious points in that skill"* (96; emphasis added). He also wrote of *"twenty other ways that well-experienced lovers could recite"* (136) and of *"twenty manner of sweet kisses"* (141). And when Shakespeare wanted to refer to an arbitrarily large number of things in a figurative rather than in a literal way, what number did he choose? Also twenty. With the exception of thousand, he used it far more often than dozen, thirty, forty, hundred, etc. In the works of Shakespeare, we find twenty swords,[328] gashes,[329] murders,[330] lies,[331] consciences,[332] husbands,[333] merchants,[334] messengers,[335] cooks,[336] orators,[337] Fallstaffs,[338] angels,[339] torches,[340] shadows,[341] kisses,[342] nose-gays,[343] glow-worms,[344] horses,[345] popish tricks,[346] and [royal, not monetary] crowns[347] (yes, I just gave twenty examples).

Spurgeon noted Shakespeare's deep fascination with the human body in motion—what she called "this marked delight in swift, nimble bodily movement" (50). "Pictures drawn from the body and bodily actions form the largest single section of all Shakespeare's images" (49). The *Arte* calls motion "the author of life" (187). It uses an intriguing trope of human runners for various metrical feet in poetry—"[N]othing can better show the quality than these runners at common games, who, setting forth from the first goal, one giveth the start speedily and perhaps before he come halfway to the other goal, decayeth his pace as a man weary and fainting; another is slow at the start, but by amending his pace keeps even with his fellow or perchance gets before him..." (159).

Spurgeon further observes that "one of the secrets of [Shakespeare's] magical style" is his capacity to "endow inanimate and motionless objects with a sense of life" (51). As Whigham and Rebhorn note, the *Arte* similarly personifies rhetorical terms (such as "the Figure of Twins" for hendiadys)—the author "transforms the vast majority of the tropes and schemes into *characters*... Sometimes the personifications seem to identify actual social types... Puttenham's personifications essentially turn life into a continual allegory" (59).

Literary studies lack a fully reliable methodology for investigating authorship claims. Physicians are encouraged to consider a broad "differential diagnosis" before arriving at a single diagnostic hypothesis that best accounts for the patient's history of illness, symptoms, physical examination, and laboratory studies. We then prescribe a course of treatment. However, if the patient fails to respond favorably to treatment, or if symptoms arise that are inconsistent with the initial diagnosis, we are taught to go back to square one and question that diagnosis. A frequent cognitive error of physicians, nevertheless, is to place undue weight on those observations that are consistent with one diagnosis, and explain away data that are not. A related "confirmatory bias" is a well-recognized danger in all scientific research—the investigator should always be mindful of the danger of selectively attending to confirmatory data that support his or her hypothesis, while downplaying, ignoring, or explaining away contradictory evidence.

The field of literary studies has not yet come to terms with its own problems of methodology. As North puts it, we abhor the "vacuum" of anonymous authorship, so that once an author receives enough of a critical mass of support, we then are in danger of engaging in circular reasoning to highlight favorable evidence, and downplay contradictory evidence. Once George Puttenham had won that critical mass of support, we entered such a phase of mind-numbing circular reasoning, where scholars wear blinders in looking for evidence to support his authorship. North is exceptional in challenging Puttenham's authorship.

Who was "Ignoto"?

Why did Harington write to the publisher Richard Field about "Putnam" as author of the *Arte*? We do not know. But we know that de Vere concealed his authorship of his best works behind another person. As I will argue, I believe that by 1591 Harington knew the truth about de Vere's authorship. Perhaps a taboo arose against mentioning de Vere's name in connection with his literary activities from the mid-1580's onward. Anonymous authorship may have been a condition for de Vere's return to court from exile in 1583. Harington was Queen Elizabeth's godson; his father's first wife was reputedly an illegitimate daughter of Henry VIII. He had the reputation of being an "impudent gadfly" at court.[348] He was known for his satirical epigrams. "We can identify few of the objects of his satire by name... but doubtless the contemporary court readily would recognize them" (xx). Harington is on record as having exposed the identity of another literary figure. He was the sole Elizabethan who blatantly violated the taboo against identifying Lady Rich as the "Stella" of Phillip Sidney's sonnet sequence, *Astrophel and Stella.*[349]

To this day, the theatrical community keeps alive what may be a displaced version of a Shakespearean name taboo in connection with one specific play--*Macbeth*. Many professional actors use the euphemism "the Scottish play" in the belief that saying *Macbeth* aloud will bring back luck. This can be compared to the possibility that the community of children have kept alive detailed "memories" of the medieval plague in the words of "Ring around the rosie" (referring to the red rings on the skin, an early symptom of the plague; "Ashes, ashes all fall down" may allude to cremation after death; "Pocket full of posie" seemingly refers to the apotropaic use of posies of herbs).[350] The intergenerationally traumatic impact of the massive number of deaths from the plague would help explain the endurance of this nursery rhyme. It would not be surprising if there were one or more deaths in de Vere's time that were believed to represent punishment of those who violated the taboo against publicly connecting de Vere with his anonymous and pseudonymous literary works. Rumors of such deaths would have powerfully enforced a taboo against naming him in connection with his "Shakespearean" plays.

I believe Harington's 1591 preface to Ariosto contains strong evidence that, by then, he knew de Vere was the author of the *Arte*. Harington referred to the author of the *Arte* as "that unknown Godfather... our *Ignoto*." "Ignoto" is Latin (and Italian) for "unknown." (It does *not* merely mean "Anonymous," as some seem to think.) This change from "Putnam" to "that unknown Godfather... our *Ignoto*" amplifies the mystery of the author's pseudonymity. Given North's findings as to the frequency of anonymity of authorship in early modern England, we might expect to find hundreds of poems subscribed "Ignoto." "Ignoto" was first used as a pseudonym in 1590, below a commendatory poem in *The Faerie Queene*. It was subscribed to only about 20 Elizabethan poems, in print or in manuscript. Why so few?

The full story of Ignoto has never been told, but it is highly relevant to the authorship of the *Arte*. Before 1590, Early English Books Online (EEBO) lists its use in English exclusively in the phrase "Ignoto Deo," from the book of Acts in the New Testament. J. Thomas Looney, who was the first to propose de Vere wrote Shakespeare's works, also recognized that "Ignoto" was another of de Vere's pen names.[351] It seems likely that de Vere borrowed that pseudonym from the Latin Vulgate translation of Acts 17:23. This verse contains St. Paul's description of coming across an altar "unto the unknown god" in Athens. Here is the verse in the Geneva translation: "For as I passed by, & behelde your devocions, I founde an altar wherein was written, UNTO THE UNKNOWN GOD, Whome ye then ignorantly worship, him shewe I unto you." In Latin, "unknown god" is "Ignoto deo."

So de Vere is identifying himself with that unknown god-- rebranded by St. Paul as the Judeo-Christian God-- in his pseudonym Ignoto. There is the additional hint that de Vere hoped, in choosing "Ignoto" as a pen name, that he too-- like the "unknown god"-- would one day be correctly identified by some latter-day St. Paul, such as Looney himself.

But there is more. I had noticed that Acts 17:28 (that is, five verses below the one I just quoted) reads "For in him we live, and move, and have our being, as also certeine of your own Poetes have said, For we are also his generacion." A Genevan marginal note offers this gloss on "Poetes"-- "As Aratus and others." The italicized phrase is the fifth line of the poem "Phaenomena," by Aratus. This illustrates, by the way, the quality of the scholarship of the Geneva Bible printed marginal notes. (Aratus was a popular Greek poet of the third century BCE.)

Is it common for secular poets to be quoted in the New Testament? I posed that question to Professor Bart Ehrman, a leading New Testament scholar at the University of North Carolina at Chapel Hill. He said Acts 17:28 is the only such instance of which he is aware. Another significant aspect of Acts 17:28 is that it is the only occurrence of the word "Poet/s" in the Geneva Bible. This may be yet another reason that de Vere, fond as he was of his Geneva Bible, decided to borrow Ignoto as one of his pen names.

Harington was alluding to this origin of the pseudonym "Ignoto" in his linking it with "that *unknown God*father." In Exodus 3:14, God answered Moses' question about God's name by replying "I am that I am." (In 1 Corinthians 15:10, St. Paul, who never lacked self-confidence, also wrote, "But by the grace of God, I am that I am.") Now, what Elizabethan author had the hubris to join St. Paul in quoting God's "I am that I am" in a letter and in a sonnet? None other than Edward de Vere—in his angry postscript to his October 30, 1584 letter to his father-in-law Lord Burghley; and also in Sonnet 121. His grandiosity in so doing is consistent with his chutzpah in using the pseudonym Ignoto.

To return to Harington. His interest in the *Arte* increases the significance of some of his other comments in his preface to his translation of Ariosto. On the first page of that preface, Harington writes the following:

"I must arm myself with the best defensive weapons I can, and if I happen to give a blow now and then in mine own defense, and as good fencers use to ward and strike at once, I must crave pardon of course, seeing our law allows that it is done *se defendo*."

Why this fencing trope? I contend it was a transparent allusion to one of the most lurid of the many scandals that marked de Vere's notorious life. While living as William Cecil's ward, de Vere, at the age of 17, killed an under-cook with his fencing sword. The coroner's inquest ruled that the servant "ran and fell upon the point of the Early of Oxford's foil" (Anderson, 35). De Vere would have been executed for this capital offence if he had been found guilty. The future Lord Burghley assisted in de Vere's legal defense, which led to de Vere being found innocent. Burghley wrote in his journal that de Vere killed the servant "se defendo"—in self-defense, which saved de Vere from execution.

"Se defendo" was *not* a common phrase in literary works. In fact, Harington's use of it in the above quotation is the *first* one cited in EEBO. And the phrase "se offendendo" in the discussion of Ophelia's death in *Hamlet* V,i,9 has been linked by Oxfordians with the same story:

It must be "se *offendendo*;" it cannot be else. For here lies the point: if I drown myself wittingly, it argues an act: and an act hath three branches: it is, to act, to do, to perform: argal, she drowned herself wittingly.

Here, as in the accusation against de Vere in 1567, the topic is a death, ostensibly by suicide (and its religious implications).

I believe Harington is making a snide *ad hominem* reference to de Vere's past scandals, in preparation for comparing the *Arte* unfavorably with Philip Sidney's *Defense of Poetry*. The fact that Harington favors Sidney over the *Arte* is consistent with Harington knowing de Vere wrote the *Arte*, since de Vere's longstanding feud with Sidney could have polarized their associates. Sidney's engagement with Burghley's daughter was broken when Burghley found a more promising match in his ward de Vere. Years later, Sidney and de Vere had their famous tennis court quarrel. (I would wonder if Sidney's death in 1586 was yet another factor that motivated de Vere to write his competing work on literary theory.)

I suspect there may be a further allusion to de Vere near the end of Harington's preface, when he returns to the *Arte*'s having slighted the significance of translators. Harington writes, "Now for those who count it such a contemptible and trifling matter to translate, I will but say to them as *M. Bartholomew Clarke* an excellent learned man, and a right good translator, saith in the matter of a prettie [clever] challenge, in his Preface (as I remember) upon the Courtier, which book he translated out of Italian into Latin." Harington knew that de Vere not only wrote the preface to that translation of Castiglione, but took the initiative to have the book published. So it may not have been coincidental that the translator Harington named was Clarke.

North cites Ruth Hughey's belief that Harington had "inside information about Oxford's authorship" (178) of one poem in the commonplace book of poems known as the Arundel Harington Manuscript. I suspect Harington similarly had inside information about de Vere's authorship of the *Arte*, as well.

In Harington's 1596 *An Apologie*, he again speaks of "*this ignoto*." We know that Harington kept the same Latin cognomen for a given person in his writings.[352] Two pages after mentioning "this ignoto," Harington mentions Richard III. Four pages after that, he cites "the rules of taming a shrew." Three pages later, he writes of riding "like a hotspurre." I wonder if Harington is hinting here that he knew about the Shakespearean plays that Ignoto was writing.

North comments that E.K.'s epistle in Edmund Spenser's 1579 *The Shepheard's Calender* begins with the words "uncouth, unkissed." North does so in order to link these words with the "passive obscurity" (52) of anonymous authorship. As I noted earlier, Shakespeare is credited with coining some 309 words that begin with "un." E.K.'s epistle coined the word "unstayed," 11 years before the first use noted in the OED. E.K. also coined "unheedie" in his gloss of a subsequent poem later in the book. In the epistle, E.K. coined two additional words: scholion and quidam. Such word usage and word coining link E.K. with Shakespeare/de Vere. Mike Hyde (2009) recently reviewed previous evidence supporting the identification of E.K. as de Vere.

In 1590, Edmund Spenser's third dedicatory sonnet in *The Faerie Queene* was addressed to the Earl of Oxford. It included a reference to "*Envy*'s poisonous bite." (The Latin proverb "Virtutis comes invidia" taught that "Envy is the companion of excellence.") Similarly, one of the prior commendatory poems refers to "a mind with *envy* fraught" and to "free my mind from *envy*'s touch." That was the poem signed "Ignoto." Again, this was the *first* use of the pseudonym Ignoto, one year before Harington referred to the author of the *Arte* as "our Ignoto."

Two poems signed "William Shakespeare" in the 1598 *Phoenix Nest* ("The unknowne Sheepheards complaint" and "Another of the same Sheepheards") were re-attributed to "Ignoto" in the 1600 *England's Helicon*. Three poems later in that 1600 book is a poem signed "Earle of Oxenford." Two other poems in *England's Helicon* were initially attributed to Walter Ralegh and Fulke Greville, respectively; but cancel slips were glued over each name, replacing them with "Ignoto."

One noteworthy example from the short list of Elizabethan "Ignoto" poems is on p. 169 of the 1601 *Loves Martyr*. The 6-line poem "The first" is printed above the 8-line poem "The Burning." They are both signed "Ignoto." This is one of 4 pages in the book that feature printer's headpieces and tailpieces. The other 3 pages are the first 2 pages of Chester's dedicatory poem; and p. 172, that contains a poem titled "Threnos." It is subscribed "William Shake-speare." (It is not well known, by the way, that "hyphenated surnames in English originated in the nineteenth century" [Murray, 2002, 180], only after a 19th-century law led wealthy men who lacked sons to require a prospective son-in-law to combine the latter's surname with his wife's, with a hyphen between. In the early modern period, by contrast, hyphenated surnames of the form Verb-noun were transparent pseudonyms.) One can make a case for pp. 169-172 constituting a single poetic work.[353] The fact that "Let the bird of loudest lay" famously lacks a title is consistent with this hypothesis. Naturally, the implication of such a hypothesis is, once again, that Ignoto and Shake-speare are the same person. If so, the many references to two becoming one in "Let the bird of loudest lay" would refer, among other things, to these two pseudonyms that de Vere used. There are some 14 key words in these two Ignoto poems that are also used in the adjacent "Shake-speare" poem, further linking them together. This hypothesis is consistent with the 1598 "Shakespeare" poems that were attributed to "Ignoto" two years later. So I would speculate that the early modern "Ignoto" poet was de Vere in every published case.[354]

J. Thomas Looney was the first to attribute the Ignoto poems in *England's Helicon* to de Vere. The eminent scholar Hyder Rollins attributes four poems from the 1614 second edition of *England's Helicon* to Ignoto. One of these 1614 poems has a direct connection with de Vere. It is the poem titled "The Sheepheards Slumber." The 1585-90 Harleian Manuscript has been called the most extensive surviving anthology of Elizabethan courtier verse. Its number 7392, folio 51, has a 28-line earlier version of "The Sheepheards Slumber" that is signed "L ox" which, as Rollins acknowledges, referred to "Lord Oxford." The fact that this poem has been attributed to "Ignoto" by Rollins, but was signed "L ox" in the Harleian Manuscript further supports the hypothesis that Ignoto and de Vere were one and the same poet.

What difference does it make, after all, *who* wrote the *Arte*? The same question is often asked of those who doubt the traditional theory of the authorship of Shakespeare's works. I would reply that it would be of enormous interest if the same person in fact wrote both the *Arte* and the works of Shakespeare. I believe that the same person did. We are depriving ourselves of significant opportunities for scholarly advances in our understanding of the works of Shakespeare by clinging to crumbling if widely accepted evidence for the legendary author. This evidence erodes considerably if we take seriously the studies of North, Mullan and others on literary anonymity. We will then have to acknowledge that the case for the traditional author of Shakespeare's works is based largely on the questionable assumption that all contemporary references to this name were indisputably references to the (front) man from Stratford rather than to a pseudonym. I have attempted to re-open the related question as to who in fact wrote *The Arte of English Poesie.* I hope further attention will be devoted to the possibility that it was Edward de Vere—"our Ignoto." If he did in fact write the *Arte*, it would give us further evidence that he published later literary works anonymously (e.g., behind the front man from Stratford). Renewed attention needs to be devoted to connections between the *Arte* and the works of Shakespeare.

William Scott's 1599 *The Model of Poesy*[355]

In 2004, Stanley Wells announced in the *Times Literary Supplement* his discovery of this important but never published Elizabethan manuscript on poetry. Wells highlighted William Scott's role as Shakespeare's first serious literary critic. In his excellent editorial apparatus, Gavin Alexander, who edited the book for its first publication, side-steps some peculiar oddities of *The Model*. For example, Alexander does not address the fact that *The Model* borrows extensively from the 1589 *Arte of English Poesie* without ever once acknowledging that earlier book. Any student or scholar who did this today would be condemned for blatant plagiarism. And Scott *does* mention by name the authors of *other* works that he cites. So failing to name an important source was atypical for Scott. If Scott knew that Puttenham wrote *The Arte*, why did he fail to mention that? What about "Shakespeare"? Once again, Scott is intriguingly silent, though he mentions "that well-conceited tragedy Richard the Second" and *The Rape of Lucrece*, from which he quotes. Alexander squarely faces this failure, but then evades the obvious question as to its meaning: "Scott does not name Shakespeare as the play's [i.e., *Richard II*'s] author at any point, but we cannot infer from this that he used the anonymous 1597 quarto [of the play]: he also fails to name Shakespeare as the author of *Lucrece*, and Shakespeare's authorship of that work was clear...' (133).

As I have explained, there are abundant internal clues in *The Arte of English Poesie* that its author was the very nobleman *The Arte* names as a great Elizabethan poet and playwright who preferred to write anonymously: Edward de Vere. There is nothing in *The Model* that contradicts the Oxfordian authorship hypothesis, while the two omissions I have emphasized do not offer any support for the traditional Stratfordian authorship hypothesis.

Marcy North points out that 16th- and early 17th-century commonplace books fail to mention Shakespeare as the author when they copy his sonnets, even when they name the other poets whose poems they copy. So here is an important precedent for Scott's failure to name Shakespeare as author of *Richard II* or of *The Rape of Lucrece*. This failure comes as no surprise to Oxfordians. We recognize that it was only with the 1623 publication of The First Folio that there was a concerted effort to invent "William Shake-speare" as author of the canon. At the time Scott wrote, in 1599, those in the know seemed to respect de Vere's wish for authorial anonymity. Yet Scott's failure to use the name "William Shakespeare" from the dedicatory epistle of *The Rape of Lucrece* hints that he does not wish to promote the use of that pseudonym.

It is curious that, despite Alexander's impressive scholarship, he does not consider the implications of Scott's failure to name *The Arte* as a primary source of his book; nor of Scott's failure to name Shakespeare as author of two of the works he discusses. Post-Stratfordians are well acquainted with the various scotomata of the Stratfordians. But here we have the opportunity to observe such a blind spot in statu nascendi.

REFERENCES

Blank, Paula, *Shakespeare and the Mismeasurement of Renaissance Man.* Ithaca, NY: Cornell University Press, 2006.
Crystal, David, *The Stories of English.* London: Penguin, 2004.
Duncan-Jones, Katherine and H.R. Woudhysen, *Shakespeare's Poems.* London: Arden, 2007.

Fowler, Alastair, *Triumphal Forms: Structural Patterns in Elizabethan Poetry*. Cambridge: Cambridge University Press, 1970.

Hammond, Paul, "Sources for Shakespeare's Sonnets 87 and 129 in *Tottel's Miscellany* and Puttenham's *The Arte of English Poesie.*" *Notes and Queries* 150: 407-410, 2003.

May, Steven, "Tudor aristocrats and the mythical 'stigma of print.'" *Renaissance Papers*. Raleigh: Southeastern Renaissance Conference, p. 11-18, 1981.

May, Steven, article on George and Richard Puttenham, *ODNB*, 2003.

Mullan, John, *Anonymity: A Secret History of English Literature*. London: Faber and Faber, 2007.

Murray, Thomas E., "The overlooked and understudied onomastic hyphen." *Names: A Journal of Onomastics* 50:173-190, 2002.

North, Marcy L., "Anonymity's revelations in *The Arte of English Poesie*. *Studies in English Literature* 39: 1-18, 1999.

North, Marcy L., *The Anonymous Renaissance: Cultures of Discretion in Tudor-Stuart England*. Chicago: Univ. of Chicago Press, 2003.

Streitberger, W.R., "Chambers on the revels office and Elizabethan theater history." *Shakespeare Quarterly* 59:185-209, 2008.

Waugaman, Richard M., "A Wanderlust Poem, Newly Attributed to Edward de Vere," *Shakespeare Matters* 7:21-23, 2007.

_____, "A Snail Poem, Newly Attributed to Edward de Vere," *Shakespeare Matters* 7:6-11, 2008.

_____, "Echoes of the 'Lamed' Section of Psalm 119 in Shakespeare's Sonnets." *Shakespeare Matters* 8:1-8 2009.

_____, "The Sternhold and Hopkins *Whole Book of Psalms* Is a Major Source for the Works of Shakespeare." *Notes & Queries* 56:595-604, 2009.

_____, "Echoes of the *Whole Book of Psalms* in Shakespeare's *1 Henry VI, Richard II,* and *Edward III. Notes & Queries* 57:359-364, 2010.

_____, "An Oxfordian Quark, or a Quirky Oxfreudian? Psalm Evidence of de Vere's Authorship of Shakespeare's Works." *The Shakespeare Oxford Newsletter* Spring issue; pp. 19-24, 2012.

_____, "Shakespeare's Sonnet 6 and the First Marked Passage in de Vere's Bible," *Shakespeare Matters,* 9:15-18, 2010.

Whigham, Frank and Wayne A. Rebhorn, *The Art of English Poesy.* Ithaca: Cornell Univ. Press, 2007.

Willcock, Gladys Doidge and Alice Walker, *The Arte of English Poesie.* Cambridge: Cambridge University Press, 1936.

Willis, Charles Murray, *Shakespeare and George Puttenham's Arte of English Poesie.* East Sussex: UPSO, 2003.

Chapter Nine

The Arte of Overturning Tradition: Did E.K.-- a.k.a. E.O. --Write the Arte of English Poesie?

A Response to Michael J. Hyde[356]

I append here my response to Michael J. Hyde, who wrote a skeptical critique of my attribution of the *Arte* to de Vere, in the same issue of the journal that originally published my work on the *Arte*. I believe many readers will share Hyde's skepticism as to my claim that de Vere wrote the *Arte*, and that my reply to him may be of more general interest.

Four centuries of tradition tell us that a certain person is known to have been the author of a work of Elizabethan literature. This "knowledge" gradually becomes inextricably intertwined with our understanding of that work of literature, bringing the printed words to life, as we form assumptions about the literary composition and its connections with the life of the author. These connections need not be extensive or definitively validated. Nevertheless, they help anchor the text in the real world of its author. All is well. Then along comes someone who tries to upset what we know. He claims that our traditional attribution is in error. And the error is alleged to be a deliberate effort by the work's actual author to mislead contemporaries and future generations into thinking someone other than the true author wrote this work. Naturally, the forces of authority and the defenders of tradition will repudiate anyone who tries to separate us from our beliefs.

This trouble-maker could be J. Thomas Looney, who infuriated the defenders of the traditional author of Shakespeare's works. In the present case, though, I have a different Elizabethan work in mind. I have been asked to respond to Michael Hyde's thoughtful comments on my contention that the *Arte of English Poesie* was written by Edward de Vere. Of course, I am no J. Thomas Looney, and I do not claim that the *Arte* rivals the Shakespearean canon in artistic importance. Nevertheless, I begin with this comparison because the issues are not only parallel, but intimately related.

Most Shakespeare scholars-- and the many people who still trust the authority of those scholars-- reject Looney's attribution of the Shakespeare canon to de Vere. Few of them will take seriously my attribution of the *Arte* to de Vere. However, those of us who recognize the likelihood of de Vere's authorship of Shakespeare's works will be more open-minded about who wrote the *Arte*. Oxfordians (and other "post-Stratfordians") already suspect that Shakspere of Stratford was at some point chosen as a front-man for the true author of the canon. So the works were not anonymous in the narrow sense of lacking the name of an ostensible author. Nor were they pseudonymous in the narrow sense of having an imaginary author's name. The First Folio of 1623, in particular, took some pains to construct a false myth about a real person who supposedly wrote these works. De Vere may have played a role in this deception. I believe he practiced a similar deception with his authorship of the commentary of "E.K." in *The Shephearde's Calender*. The slender thread on which the traditional attribution of the *Arte* hangs is John Harington's 1590 letter to Richard Field. Why is it so far-fetched to imagine that de Vere played some role in a deliberate effort to falsely attribute the *Arte* to George Puttenham, just as he did with the attribution of his Shakespeare canon to the man from Stratford?

My article speculated that Harington was alluding to de Vere in his "se defendo" fencing trope, in his preface to Ariosto. It was a nasty dig at one of the scandals in de Vere's past. It was not the only time that Harington skewered de Vere. Harington's epigrams were too inflammatory to be published before his death in 1610. In seven of his 400 epigrams, Harington satirizes de Vere as "Caius."[357] Enacting Iago's role, Harington accuses de Vere's wife of infidelity—specifically, he claims she became pregnant with another man's child while de Vere was abroad.[358] Another epigram claims de Vere got Ann Vavasour pregnant in a privy.[359]

A frequent assumption about anonymous or pseudonymous authors is that they hope to be discovered and given credit for their works. Such an author would be likely to sprinkle his or her works with reliable clues as to his or her real identity. But what if de Vere wanted his authorship to remain concealed? In that case, we can reasonably expect that he planted *false* clues about his identity in the *Arte*. I am not certain that Hyde has fully considered this possibility, since I gather that he takes the "self references and self quotations" of the *Arte* at face value, despite the efforts of my article to question this very assumption.

There is often an insidious and unrecognized circularity in false authorship attributions. For example, Stratfordians routinely assume Shakespeare must have attended the grammar school in Stratford, and that it must have had a fine curriculum. I hope we will not emulate the Stratfordians as we re-examine authorship of the *Arte*. Hyde writes that "The author of the *Arte* tells us repeatedly that he wrote "Partheniades," so to displace Puttenham [as author of] the *Arte* is also to claim that de Vere wrote the former poem in 1579 for which there is no evidence." This reasoning seems circular, because it assumes the very point in contention—namely, authorship of the *Arte*. It is not logical to assume the authorship of "Partheniades" has been proven because the anonymous author of the *Arte* says he wrote it.[360] As I noted in my article, I am unaware of any independent evidence that attributes these poems to Puttenham. They are anonymous. Those who challenge the traditional authorship of Shakespeare's works are held to a different standard of evidence than is the traditional theory. This double standard represents an abuse of the authority of tradition. But it is so widespread because of the weakness of the Stratfordian case. We need to avoid it.

Hyde believes that my article's "attempts to cast doubt on the scholarship of Marcy North, Steven May, Charles W. Willis, and... Frank Whigham and Wayne Rebhorn are diversionary..." I hope I will be permitted to disagree with other scholars when I feel I have grounds for doing so, and when my disagreement with them is central to the thesis of my article. As it happens, my agreement with North outweighs our differences. North has launched a cogent challenge against traditional Elizabethan authorship assumptions. Her book has not received the serious attention that it deserves. North rejects the attribution of the *Arte* to Puttenham,[361] an attribution which is endorsed by May, Whigham, and Rebhorn. I assume that all of them would reject Willis's attribution of the works of Shakespeare to Puttenham. So readers should not be misled into assuming that these five scholars agree among themselves.

Hyde believes that the *Arte*'s references to de Vere prove that he could not have been the author, since these references are in the third person. But writing of himself in the third person would be an obvious ploy if de Vere wished to conceal his authorship. As with Stratfordians who rest their traditional belief on the supposed authority of the First Folio, textual evidence is taken at face value, ignoring plentiful signs that Elizabethans delighted in deceit. North finds in the *Arte* a subtle and complex discussion of the courtier's art of deception. She believes we have not sufficiently appreciated the implications of deception in the anonymity of the *Arte*. As I wrote, "North shows compellingly that the author of the *Arte*, by remaining anonymous, added further layers of complexity to *the contradictory advice he gave to the reader about literary anonymity*" (emphasis added). So I do not join Hyde in taking at face value the *Arte*'s advice that authors should sign their works.

Hyde writes, "No evidence is offered for speculations... that de Vere published early verse in the *Paradise of Daintie Devises* ...in order to win his license to travel to Europe." Due to space limitations, I was not able to rehearse the evidence of my 2007 article, which attributes this poem to de Vere. The poem is titled, "A young Gentleman, willing to travel into forreygne partes, being intreated to staie in England: Wrote as followeth." It is published immediately after three poems signed by de Vere with his initials, "E.O." Its rhyme scheme is like the first two: ABABCC. The *Arte* especially favors such six-verse stanzas as being "very pleasant to the eare" (80).

After de Vere defied the Queen and tried to visit the Continent without her permission in 1574, an anonymous report said "The desire of travel is not yet quenched in [de Vere], though he dare not make any motion unto Her Majesty that he may with her favor accomplish the said desire" (quoted in Anderson, 72). As I wrote in 2007,[362] "Even 'intreated' in the title speaks volumes. The Queen gave commands—she did not entreat" (21). I speculated that this poem was only published in 1585 because "de Vere had to choose his battles with the Queen, since he repeatedly pushed her too far by his defiance. Publishing this poem any sooner might have rubbed her face in a public reminder of his unauthorized trip to Flanders, along with his other acts of insubordination" (21). I speculated that de Vere left this poem anonymous, "suggesting a compromise between conflicting wishes to make it public, but to avoid angering the Queen. It is instructive to notice and ponder such examples of de Vere playing with anonymity, moving back and forth across the line of identifying himself to his readers" (21).

Hyde says that if de Vere wrote the *Arte*, "there should be notice of the discussion of figures [of rhetoric] in other known or suspected works by de Vere." Hyde asks, for example, why we do not find allusions to classical rhetorical figures in E.K.'s glosses on *The Shephearde's Calender*. Excessive certainty about authorship creates blind spots for contradictory evidence. I gather Hyde has not noticed the many parallels between the explicit discussion of rhetoric in the *Arte* and that in E.K.'s commentary, which uses several of the same classical rhetorical terms that are "Englished" in the *Arte*.

In the commentary on January, E.K. refers to "Epanorthosis"[363] and "Paronomasia."[364] In February, we find "a certaine Icon or Hypotyposis"; the *Arte* speaks of "your figure of *icon*, or Resemblance by Imagery and Portrait"; it calls Hypotyposis "the Counterfeit Representation." The glosses on March include "Periphrasis." This term was also used by the *Arte,* which translates it as "the Figure of Ambage,"[365] and links periphrasis with "dissimulation." It illustrates this rhetorical figure with an excerpt of a poem the author wrote. He explains that the poem indirectly means "her Majesty's person, which we would seem to hide, leaving her name unspoken, to the intent the reader should guess at it; nevertheless upon [consideration] the matter did so manifestly disclose it, as any simple judgment might easily perceive by whom it was meant." The author may be alluding indirectly to his self-concealment when he criticizes poets who "blabbed out" what they should have dealt with more "discreetly" by ambage, so that "now there remaineth for the reader somewhat to study and guess upon."

In April, we find "Calliope, one of the nine Muses. Other[s] say, that shee is *the Goddesse of Rhetorick*"[366] (emphasis added). May includes "a careful Hyperbaton," which the *Arte* calls "the Trespasser." The *Arte* warns that this figure is often used in a "foul and intolerable" manner, which may explain why E.K. qualifies Spenser's use of it as "careful." May also explains a passage as being "an Epiphonema," which the *Arte* calls "the Surclose of Consenting Close." July offers "Synecdochen," called "Synecdoche, or the Figure of Quick Conceit" in the *Arte*, which says "it encumbers the mind with a certain imagination what it may be that is meant, and not expressed." Again, we may think of the self-concealment of the author. October offers "An Ironical Sarcasmus, spoken in *derision*," which the *Arte* calls "the Bitter Taunt... when we *deride*" (emphasis added). I hope this evidence will satisfy Hyde that E.K. shared with the author of the *Arte* a deep interest in explicating terms of rhetoric to his readers.

Hyde is silent on the earlier identification of E.K. as Spenser's friend Edmund Kirke. Most Spenser scholars now assume E.K. was probably just a fiction invented by Spenser himself. They sometimes react to any remaining doubts about the identity of E.K. with the time-honored evasion, "What difference would it make anyway??" It does make a difference if de Vere deliberately concealed his authorship behind the initials of Spenser's close college friend Edmund Kirke. It would increase the likelihood that de Vere played a role in what may have been Harington's similarly deliberate false attribution of the *Arte* to "Putnam." Further, it would make a world of difference to the question of who wrote Shakespeare's canon. Is there any textual evidence in *The Shephearde's Calender* that E.K. concerned himself with concealed authorship? Indeed, there is. In fact, the very first of E.K.'s glosses concerns the name Colin Cloute—"a name not greatly used, and yet have I sene a Poesie of M. Skeletons under that title. But indeede the word Colin is Frenche, and used of the French Poete Marot... *Under which name this Poete* (i.e., the anonymous author of *The Shephearde's Calender*) *secretly shadowed* (obscured, concealed) *himself*, as sometime did Virgil under the name of Tityrus" (emphasis added). Is this first gloss E.K.'s way of alerting careful readers to the possibility of self-concealment on E.K.'s part? Perhaps so. The self-concealment of an author also appears in E.K.'s comments on September. There, he says that Gabriel Harvey sometimes wrote "under counterfayt names."

Naturally, I am pleased that Hyde shares my excitement about further research on the Ignoto poems. I am grateful to Michael Hyde for his close reading of my essay, and for this opportunity to strengthen the case my article makes for de Vere's authorship of the *Arte of English Poesie.*

CONCLUSION

Have I proven that Edward de Vere wrote the works of
Shakespeare? No. But then, neither have the traditional
Stratfordians proven their traditional authorship theory. I
have instead simply suggested a likely expansion of the
works written by "William Shake-Speare," in the
knowledge that de Vere's authorship of these works is a
theory that keeps gaining in evidence and plausibility. One
of the many benefits of developing a more accurate
inventory of the literary works of Edward de Vere is that
we then can more deeply appreciate the developmental
trajectory of his phenomenal literary genius, rather than
accept the implausible Stratfordian assumption that he
began writing at the height of his literary powers. Once we
are willing to relinquish our strong emotional attachment
to the appealing legend of the simple man from Stratford
becoming the world's greatest writer, we can enjoy the
literary works of Shakespeare even more than we did
before, as we learn more about the genius who actually
wrote them.

ENDNOTES

[1] *Shakespeare in Court*. Kindle Single, 2014.

[2] See Richard M. Waugaman, "What Are the Implications of the Spelling 'Shake-Speare' in Ben Jonson's 1616 Folio?" *Shakespeare Oxford Society Newsletter* 52(3):36 (2016)

[3] Since I do not review de Vere's life story in this book, the reader is encouraged to consult Mark Anderon, *"Shakespeare" by Another Name: The Life of Edward de Vere, Earl of Oxford, the Man Who Was Shakespeare.* New York, Gotham Books, 2005.

[4] One important exception was A. Bronson Feldman--see A.B. Feldman, *Hamlet Himself.* New York, iUniverse, 2010.

[5] Roger Stritmatter, *Edward de Vere's Geneva Bible,* Northampton, MA: Oxenford Press, 2001.

[6] Richard M. Waugaman and Roger Stritmatter, "Who Was 'William Shakespeare'? We Propose He Was Edward de Vere," *Scandinavian Psychoanalytic Review* 32:2 (2009), pp. 105-115.

[7] I have given many examples of these allusions to marked passages in the following articles,: "The Sternhold and Hopkins Psalter is a major source for the works of Shakespeare," *Notes & Queries* 56:4 (2009), pp. 595-604; "Echoes of the 'Lamed' Section of Psalm 119 in Shakespeare's Sonnets." *Shakespeare Matters* 8:4 (2009), pp. 1, 8-9, 27; "Psalm Allusions in Shakespeare's *1 Henry VI, Richard II,* and *Edward III* , *Notes & Queries* 57:3 (2010), pp. 359-364 ; "The Discovery of a Major New Literary Source for Shakespeare's Works in the de Vere Geneva Bible." *Brief Chronicles: The Interdisciplinary Journal of the Shakespeare Fellowship* 2 (2010), pp. 109-120; "Shakespeare's Sonnet 6 and the First Marked Passage in de Vere's Bible." *Shakespeare Matters* 9:3 (2010), pp. 15-18; "*Titus Andronicus,* the Psalms, and Edward de Vere's Bible" *The Oxfordian* 13 (2011), pp. 34-49; "The Sternhold and Hopkins *Whole Book of Psalms* Offers Crucial Evidence of de Vere's Authorship of the Works of Shakespeare." *Brief Chronicles* 3 (2011), pp. 213-234; "Biblical Sources for Sonnets 24 and 33, and for *Henry VIII*: Implications for de Vere's Authorship," Brief Chronicles 4 (2012-2013), pp. 73-87; "The Source for *Remembrance of Things Past* in

Shakespeare's Sonnet 30." *Shakespeare Matters* 12:1 (2013), pp. 1, 15-16.

[8] Psalms 6, 12, 25, 30, 51, 61, 65, 66, 67, 77, 103, 137, 139, and 146 are so marked. Psalms 8, 11, 15, 23, 31, and 130 are marked in other ways.

[9] Hannibal Hamlin had already discovered some of these echoes, but there are still more in the WBP translation. On the crucial topic of Shakespeare's largely neglected intertextuality with the Bible, see Hannibal Hamlin, *The Bible in Shakespeare*, Oxford, Oxford University Press, 2013. In his book, Hamlin was kind enough to cite my work on the Whole Book of Psalms.

[10] Diana Price, *Shakespeare's Unorthodox Biography*, Santa Barbara, Praeger, 2000.

[11] Irving Janis, *Groupthink: Psychological Studies of Policy Decisions and Fiascoes,* Boston, Wadsworth, 1982.

[12] Sidney Colvin, ed., *Letters of John Keats to his Family and Friends*, Cambridge, Cambridge University Press,1891, p. 48. Keats wrote this letter soon after seeing Edmund Kean act in Shakespeare's *Richard III.*

[13] Tom Siegfried, *Science News* 181(4):2, 2012.

[14] Marcy North, *The Anonymous Renaissance: Cultures of Discretion in Tudor-Stuart England*, Chicago, University of Chicago Press, 2003.

[15] "The 1574 *Mirour for Magistrates* Is a Possible Source of "Feath'red King' in Shakespeare's 'The Phoenix and the Turtle,'" *Cahiers Élisabéthains* 85:67-72, 2014.

[16] The Folger Shakespeare Library hosted a conference on "Shakespeare and the Problem of Biography" on April 3-5, 2014. David Ellis's book was not mentioned by any of the presenters. But they acknowledged the lack of fit between Shakspere's life and the literary works of Shakespeare. Presenters included Brian Cummings, Margreta de Grazia, Katherine Ducan-Jones, Stephen Greenblatt, Andrew Hadfield, Graham Holderness, and Lois Potter.

[17] David Ellis, *The Truth About William Shakespeare: Fact, Fiction and Modern Biographies,* Edinburgh, Edinburgh University Press, 2012, p. 11.

[18] David Ellis, 2012, p. 177.

[19] Bruce Danner, "The Anonymous Shakespeare: Heresy,

Authorship, and the Anxiety of Orthodoxy," in Janet Wright Starner and Barbara Howard Traister, eds., *Anonymity in Early Modern England: What's in a Name?*, Ashgate, 2011, p. 215.

[20] Ibid., p. 156.

[21] Ibid., p. 144.

[22] Ibid., p. 147.

[23] Ibid., p. 155.

[24] Ibid., p. 156.

[25] Ibid., p. 152.

[26] Stephen Greenblatt, *Will in the World: How Shakespeare Became Shakespeare*, New York, Norton, 2004.

[27] Richard M. Waugaman, "The Bisexuality of Shakespeare's Sonnets and Implications for De Vere's Authorship." *The Psychoanalytic Review* 97:4 (2010), pp. 859-879.

[28] However, Fred Schurink, in "An Unnoticed Early Reference to Shakespeare," *Notes & Queries* 53:1 (2006), pp. 72-75, drew attention to a 1628 work that suggests "Shake-speare" was a pen name. Thomas Vicars referred to "that famous poet who takes his name from shaking and spear" ["celebrem illum poeta qui a quassatione et hasta nomen habet"] (in his *Cheiragogia Manuductio ad Artem Rhetoricam*. London, Augustini Matthews, Third Edition, p. 70). One wonders if this early allusion to Shakespeare remained "unnoticed" until 2006 because it casts doubt on the traditional authorship theory.

[29] In Thomas A. Pendleton's review of the 2013 *Shakespeare Beyond Doubt*, edited by Paul Edmondson and Stanley Wells, he strongly praises the book, while expressing a "critical" reservation that "there is nowhere in the book a direct, forceful, succinct presentation of this evidence" (p. 26) that Shakspere wrote Shakespeare. Pendleton then gives his version of this supposed evidence, apparently unaware that each "fact" he cites has been challenged with plausible, contrasting interpretations of its meaning; in *Shakespeare Newsletter*, 63:1, pp. 25-26, 28, 2013.

[30] Quoted in Jack Lynch, *Becoming Shakespeare*, New York, Walker & Co., 2007, p. 243.

[31] Reproduced here:bbc.co.uk/arts/yourpaintings/paintings/the-infant-shakespeare-attended-by-nature-and-the-passions-54937

[32] Plato, *The Collected Dialogues*, E. Hamilton and H. Cairns, eds., New York, Bollingen Foundation, 1961, p. 8.

[33] Ibid., p. 220-221.

[34] Reprinted in *Shakespeare's Dramatic Works*, Vol.1, Boston, Phillips and Sampson, 1848, p. xlvii.

[35] Jack Lynch, *Becoming Shakespeare*, New York, Walker & Co., 2007, pp. 237-238.

[36] Sidney Lee, *A Life of William Shakespeare*, New York, Macmillan, 1898, p. 365.

[37] Ibid., p. 372.

[38] Ibid., p. 30.

[39] Max Weber, *The Protestant Ethic and the Spirit of Capitalism*, London, Allen & Unwin, 1930.

[40] Augustus Ralli, *History of Shakespearean Criticism*, New York, Humanities Press, 1932/1965, vol. II, p. 128 .

[41] Anonymous, review of Greenwood. *Times Literary Supplement,* 1909.

[42] Samuel Schoenbaum, *William Shakespeare: A Compact Documentary Life*, Oxford, Oxford University Press, 1977, p. x.

[43] Ibid., p. xi.

[44] In Samuel Schoenbaum, *Shakespeare's Lives,* London, Clarendon Press, 1991, p. 133.

[45] Ibid., p. 225. There is wonderful word-play here. "Embassy" means "to deliver a message," from the Latin "ambactus," or "servant." "Bent" means curved, as in "bending down"; it also means "resolute." "Stoop" means "to lower the body"; also "to bow to superior authority"; "to submit to something burdensome"; "to condescend to some position or action below one's rightful dignity"; and, finally, of a hawk or other raptor, "to descend swiftly on its prey, or to the lure." De Vere used that last meaning in "In Prayse of Snayle," which I discuss in Chapter Four. In fact, he used the phrase "can stoope to every stale." "Stale" means a "lure" used to train hawks to hunt. So, in the complex mixture of submission and defiance in these two improvised lines, de Vere hinted that the dropped glove was equivalent to a lure used to train a hawk into submission, or even to "lure" de Vere into a flirtation with the Queen.

[46] Ibid., p. 226.

[47] Quoted in Schoenbaum, Ibid., p. 225.

[48] Eugene Rimmel, *The Book of Perfumes*, London, Chapman and Hall, 1817, p. 202.

49 Ibid., p. 440.
50 Paul Edmondson and Stanley Wells, eds, *Shakespeare Beyond Doubt: Evidence, Argument, Controversy*, Cambridge, Cambridge University Press, 2013. For a rebuttal, see John M. Shahan and Alexander Waugh, eds., *Shakespeare Beyond Doubt? Exposing an Industry in Denial,* Tamarac, FL, Lumina Press, 2013.

51 For a contrasting opinion, see Richard Paul Roe, *The Shakespeare Guide to Italy: Retracing the Bard's Unknown Travels*, New York, Harper, 2011.
52 But see John Lord Campbell, *Shakespeare's Legal Acquirements Considered*, London, John Murray, 1859.
53 Stuart Gillespie *Shakespeare's Books: A Dictionary of Shakespeare's Sources*. New York, Continuum, 2001.
54 Roger Stritmatter, "A law case in verse: *Venus and Adonis* and the authorship question." *Tennessee Law Review* 72(1):171-219, 2004.
55 Ovid *Tristia* Book I, S.G. Owen, ed. Oxford: Clarendon Press, 1903.
56 Charlton Ogburn (in *The Mysterious William Shakespeare,* McLean, VA: EPM. Publications, 1984, is one of many Oxfordians who have proposed that de Vere had a hand in the "Golding" *Metamorphoses*. See also Charlton Ogburn, "The How Many Guises of Edward de Vere, *Shakespeare Oxford Newsletter*, 15(4):1-5, 1979. In my opinion, he stops short of giving de Vere his rightful credit for this entire translation. I suspect it would have been too distasteful to his uncle Arthur Golding to collaborate in it, and that they would have been too much at cross purposes to have agreed on how to English Ovid. Gordon Braden, in his *The Classics and English Renaissance Poetry* (New Haven: Yale, 1978) comments on the "otiose" "doubling of adjectives" in this translation. As though unwittingly helping build the case for the youthful de Vere as translator, Braden criticizes the inaccurate translations and *childish* diction.
57 Early English Books Online. I rely on its database extensively here, so I must acknowledge that it includes the searchable text of only some 50,000 books. Unfortunately, its database is incomplete, so any conclusions based on it are provisional. Further, it does not always provide an accurate search of words and phrases in the ostensibly searchable texts.

[58] "Ye have yet another manner of speech when ye will seem to make two of one not thereunto constrained, which therefore we call the Figure of Twins, the Greeks *hendiadys*" (261).

[59] See "*The Arte of English Poesie:* The Case for Edward de Vere's Authorship." *Brief Chronicles: The Interdisciplinary Journal of the Shakespeare Fellowship* 2:121-141, 2010; and "The Arte of Overturning Tradition: Did E.K.—a.k.a. E.O.—Write *The Arte of English Poesie?*." *Brief Chronicles: The Interdisciplinary Journal of the Shakespeare Fellowship* 2:260-266, 2010.

[60] "when one thing of itself entire is diversely laid open…This also is rather poetical than otherwise in use" (83). By the way, it is relevant that the etymology of "secretary" involves keeping the secrets of one's employer. In the case of Angel Day, this may have included secretly offering his allonym to de Vere.

[61] Philadelphia: Paul Dry Books, 2000. It is this Nims edition of the 1567 translation that I have used throughout this essay.

[62] *Ovid's Changing Worlds: English Metamorphoses, 1567-1632.* Oxford: Oxford University Press, 2001.

[63] E.g., by Marcy North in *The Anonymous Renaissance*, Chicago: University of Chicago Press, 2003.

[64] Thomas Powell referred to "our English Ovid" in 1603, as did "C.N." in 1620.

[65] In "O'er Green My Bad," in *Shakespeare Oxford Fellowship Newsletter* 21(2):2-5, 1985.

[66] *Ovid Recalled,* Cambridge: Cambridge University Press, 1955.

[67] Mark Anderson reports the tantalizing fact that Edward Dowden wrote that Coxeter thought de Vere translated Ovid (see G.M. Bowen, "A Shakespeare Allulsion Continued?" in *Shakespearean Authorship Review* 7:12, 1962).

[68] Richard M. Waugaman, "Edward de Vere Was the Translator of the 1570 *A Ritch Storehouse or Treasurie for Nobilitie and Gentlemen* by Johann Sturm." *Brief Chronicles* (in press). That essay further expands my study of de Vere's use of hendiadys from 1565-1570.

[69] "Hendiadys and *Hamlet*." *PMLA* 96(2):168-193, 1981. I am most grateful to Colin Burrow for directing me to this classic article, and for his suggestions on the work of Sturm.

[70] In *The Classics and English Renaissance Poetry* , New Haven: Yale University Press, 1978, Chapter 1, "Golding's Ovid," 1-54.

[71] I do not claim this was an original trope with de Vere. One need only recall the earlier editions of the *Mirror for Magistrates.*

[72] In Karen Newman and Jane Tylus (eds.), *Early Modern Cultures of Translation,* Philadelphia: University of Pennsylvania Press, 2015; Chap. 2, "Translating the Rest of Ovid: The Exile Poems," pp. 45-55.

[73] *Thinking in Circles: An Essay on Ring Composition.* New Haven: Yale, 2010.

[74] He preferred the older spelling, "Oxenford."

[75] It later became the name of a department of the British Civil Service.

[76] It later became the name of a department of the British Civil Service.

[77] Jan Cole discovered that "Golding" mentioned Vulcano. "An Unnoticed Source for Prospero's Island and Caliban in Golding's Translation of Ovid's *Metamorphosis*" - DVS Newsletter vol. 20(3), 2013, 18-19.☐☐☐☐☐☐☐☐☐

[78] Originally published in *Shakespeare Oxford Society Newsletter* 49(1):9-10 (2013).

[79] *The Pathe Way to Perfectness.* London: Thomas Purfoote, 1569.

[80] *Shakespeare's Imagery and What It Tells Us.* Cambridge: Cambridge University Press, 1935.

[81] *Monstrous Adversary: The Life of Edward de Vere, 17th Earl of Oxford.* Liverpool: Liverpool University Press, 2003. See also Nelson's website for list of spelling variants from de Vere's letters.

[82] Douglas Bruster describes Shakespeare's idiosyncratic spellings in his "Shakespearean Spellings and Handwriting and the Additional Passages Printed in the 1602 *Spanish Tragedy*" *Notes & Queries* 60(3):420-424. Bruster's article unintentionally provides powerful support for de Vere's authorship of the Shakespeare canon. Bruster describes 24 categories of spelling variants that, although not unique to Shakespeare, in aggregate help set him apart from other Elizabethan writers. A search of the spellings in de Vere's extant letters showed examples of nearly all of the 24 categories that characterize "Shakespeare."

[83] By contrast, Golding used "owt" only a total of 56 times, compared with 10,389 uses of "out," according to EEBO. So Golding used the "owt" variant only 5% of the time; de Vere used it 78% of the time, according to his extant letters. Further, the 1567

Metamorphoses substitutes "w" for "u" in abowt, clowt, dowt, rowt, showt, sowth, spowt, stowt, uncowth, and withowt. Four of these spellings occur in no other EEBO book in 1567; the others occur in only one to three other books, but three of these spellings are found in de Vere's letters (especially dowt, which occurs 22 times in them).

[84] Did someone persuade him to reverse the "e" and "w" in "dwe" and "trwe"? I suspect that de Vere regarded the letter "w" as "uu"; after all, that is how we pronounce the letter: "double u." So "dwe" represented "duue"; "trwe" represented "truue." Bruster described unusual double vowels as typical of Shakespeare's idiosyncratic spelling habits.

[85] "Man's estate" occurs twice in the *Metamorphoses*.

[86] This word is found in EEBO only twice in the 1560's. But "Shakespeare" was fond of words beginning "un-". (Bill Bryson, *Shakespeare: The World as Stage*. New York: Atlas Books, 2007, 114).

[87] In the 1596 commendatory poem to *The Faerie Queene* by "Ignoto" (de Vere), "taste" is also a trope.

[88] Tomlin notes the similarity with the 1567 *Metamorphoses* phrase about Daedulus in the maze: "the meanes to *winde* himselfe well *out*."

[89] Cf. 1567 *Metamorphoses* "And *fertile fields* may *fruitfull Harvests yeelde*." Later, the *Metamorphoses* has "the *feeldes* which laden were with *frutefull Harvest*."

[90] Ie., painstaking

[91] "like a Snayle" also occurs in the 1567 *Metamorphoses*.

[92] The last line of Ignoto's 1596 poem is "Then looke you give your hoast his utmost *dew*." Note once again that unusual spelling of "due."

[93] Cf. the 1596 poem by "Ignoto," which similarly warns that "a mind with envy fraught" and "envies tuch" should not lessen praise of the literary work in question. Likewise, Spenser's 1596 dedicatory sonnet to de Vere entreated him to help protect Spenser's poem from "foule Envies poisnous bit[e]."

[94] I am grateful to Colin Burrows for his helpful suggestions for this article.

[95] See Susan Doran, *Elizabeth I and Her Circle*, 179.

[96][96] Colin Burrow, Chap. 27, Shakespeare. In Patrick Cheney and

Philip Hardie (eds.), *The Oxford History of Classical Reception in English Literature.* Vol. 2 (1558-1660). Donna B. Hamilton, *Virgil and the Tempest: Politics of Imitation,* (Columbus, OH: Ohio State University Press) also discusses Sturm in connection with Shakespeare (11-18).

[97] Lewis W. Spitz and Barbara Sher Tinsley, *Johann Sturm on Education.* St. Louis: Concordia, 1995.
p. 374 note 64.

[98] Cf. Robin Fox, *Shakespeare's Education: Schools, Lawsuits, Theater and the Tudor Miracle.* Bucholz, Germany: Laugwitz Verlag, 2012.

[99] In their valuable edition of Sturm, Spitz and Tinsley refer to the translator merely as "T.B.," and do not speculate as to his identity. They call his translation "charming" (133), and they quote several lines of it.

[100] See Robert Sean Brazil, *Angel Day: The English Secretary and Edward de Vere, Seventeenth Earl of Oxford.* Seattle, WA: Cortical Output, 2013.

[101] In his English translation of Johann Sturm's *A Ritch Storehouse.*

[102] Edited by Frank Whigham and Wayne A. Rebhorn. Ithaca: Cornell University Press, 2007.

[103] "Greek Rhetorical Terminology in Puttenham's *The Arte of English Poesie." Transactions and Proceedings of the American Philological Association.* 45:111-128, 1914.

[104] Early English Books Online

[105] G.W. Pigman, "Versions of Imitation in the Renaissance." *Renaissance Quarterly* 33:1-32, 1980. I am grateful to Colin Burrow for bringing Pigman's article to my attention.

[106] Nelson calls this particular spelling "wildly egregious" (65). (Tut, tut, Shake-speare!)

[107] "Apploy'd" was used once, in 1643.

[108] "Howre" is found twice in de Vere's letters.

[109] The ever helpful Nelson writes that "Many [spelling] variants [in de Vere's letters] result from the substitution of 'w' for 'u' (64)." E.g., cowld, showld, and wowld.

[110] Sometimes, in a long series, such as "Between *two* hawks, which flies the higher pitch;/ Between *two* dogs, which hath the deeper mouth;? Between *two* blades, which bears the better temper;/ Between *two* horses, which doth bear him best;/ Between *two* girls,

which hath the merriest eye" (1 Henry VI, ii.iv.11-15

[111] De Vere did not consider one to be a number.

[112] Ancient Hebrew also has the dual number. For example, the dual form of the verb, rather than the plural, is used when speaking of a person's two legs (Rabbi Joshua Habermann, personal communication, July 2, 2016).

[113] I am grateful to Elisabeth P. Waugaman for this observation.

[114] Cf. de Vere coining the word "turquify" as meaning "transform," as described above.

[115] See "Hendiadys and *Hamlet*." PMLA 96(2)168-193, 1981. I am most grateful to Colin Burrow for directing me to this classic article, and for his suggestions on the work of Sturm.

[116] The second of 34 instances of this word pair in EEBO.

[117] The third of 275 instances in EEBO.

[118] Cf. "good and virtuous" in *Macbeth* IV.iii.23; "good and loyal" in the same play, IV.iii.97; "good and gracious" in *Timon* I.i.68; "good and galant" in *Tempest* V.i.269.

[119] The first of 22 uses, but "tedious *and* troublesome" was a commonplace. Still, an instance of de Vere fashioning something new out of old material.

[120] Cf. "rude and shallow" in *Henry V* I.i.57; "rude and wildly" in *Comedy of Errors* V.i.90; "rude and merciless" in *2 Henry VI* IV.iiii.33; "rude and savage" in *LLL*; "IV.iii.233; and "rude and bold" in *MV* II.ii.174.

[121] Later, he writes "barren and void," the third of 27 uses in EEBO.

[122] Unique in EEBO. There are no instances of the related "barren and dishonest." Shakespeare coined more than 300 words beginning "un-." Cf. "barren and bereft" in Richard II III.iii.86.

[123] First of 18 uses in EEBO.

[124] First of three uses in EEBO.

[125] Third of 145 uses in EEBO. Cf. "due and just" in *Pericles* V.iii.98; "due and wary" in *MM* IV.i.37; "due and forfeit" in *MV* IV.i.38.

[126] Cf. "use and counsel" in Shakespeare's *1 Henry IV*, I.iii.20; "use and liberty" in *MM* I.iv.66; "use and wearing" in *Timon* V.i.157; and "use and fair advantage" in *TGV* II.iv.63. Likewise, "art and practise" in *MM* I.i.12; "device and practise" in *HVIII* I.i.238; "baits and practise" in *Coriolanus* IV.i.35.

[127] Cf. "dern [concealed, solitary] and painful" in *Pericles* III,

Prologue, 15.

[128] It is possible that some of the works dedicated to de Vere were actually written by him—another use of an allonym.

[129] Cf. "slavish weeds and servile thoughts" in *Titus*, II.i.18.

[130] Cf. "manners and beauty" in *Othello* II.i.249; cf. "state and inclination" in *RII*, III.ii.195.

[131] Cf. "learned and well-beloved" in *HVIII* II.iv.256; "learned and valiant" in *TN* I.v.241; cf. "politic and safe" in Lear

[132] Cf. "noble and natural" in *Cymbeline* III.v.160; "noble and renowned" in *MM* III.i.232-233; "noble and well-warranted" in *MM* V.i.277; "noble and true-hearted" in *Lear* I.ii.121; "noble and approved" in *Othello* I.iii.87; "noble and chaste" in *I Henry IV* I.ii.28. In each case, another favorable adjective highlights and intensifies the positive connotation of "noble."

[133] Cf. "name and fame" in *2 Henry IV* II.iv.70; "name and quality" in IV.i.90 of the same play; "name and birth" in *Cymbeline* I.i.32; "name and power" in *2 Henry VI* I.iv.26; "name and credit" in *Shrew* IV.ii.112; "name and estimation" in *I Henry IV* V.i.99. As with "noble," "name" leads to positive associations for de Vere.

[134] Cfl. "manner and form" in *LLL* I.i.201, 204; "degree and form" in *Henry V* IV.i.242; "shapes and forms" in *T&C* V.iii.13.

[135] Cf. "judgment and reason" in *TN* III.ii.12.

[136] Cf. "wisely and truly" in *JC* III.iii.15-16.

[137] Cf. "old and foolish" in *Lear* IV.vii.97; "gross and foolish" in *WT* III.ii.214; "foul and foolish" in *Othello* I.i.154 and 155 (i.e., repeated in these two lines, not enjambed).

[138] Cf. "voice and utterance" in *JC* III.i.281.

[139] Cf. "Nature and Fortune" in *KJ* III.i.52

[140] Note that three of these pairs including the word *writing*.

[141] Cf. the nearly identical hendiadys "virtue and obedience" in *Shrew* V.ii.130, and also in *Lear* II.i.122. Cf. also "virtue and nobility" in *Titus* I.i.93;

[142] Cf. "gravity and learning" in Henry *VIII* III.i.82 and in *MWW* III.i.51; "gravity and patience" in the latter play, III.i.48; "gravity and stillness" in *Othello* II.iii.190

[143] "'A New 1569 Poem by Arthur Golding,' Re-attributed to Edward de Vere." *Shakespeare Oxford Society Newsletter* 49(1):9-10 (2013).

[144] Originally published in *Shakespeare Matters* 7(1):21-23, 2007.

With few exceptions, I have retained the original spelling of the poems reproduced in this book. Although I recognize that this creates a stumbling block for many readers, scholarly work on Elizabethan literature benefits greatly from using the original spelling. On the other hand, I have followed normal editorial practice in modernizing the letters "u," "v," and "i," when their original spelling would create undue hardship for the reader.

[145] wander freely

[146] high-minded; aspiring; lofty

[147] fortune; luck; chance

[148] formerly

[149] to be in a troubled state of mind; "care and carkes" appears in another unsigned poem in the 1596 edition ("He renounceth all the affects of Love")

[150] one meaning is an old worn out shoe-- cf. buckled [bent up or wrinkled] shoe in the next line

[151] rather than

[152] since the 14th century, three pagans, three Jews, and three Christians who embodied the ideal of chivalry; they were a popular subject for Renaissance masques, as satirized in *Loves Labours Lost*

[153] to display a heraldic charge on one's shield; to have as a quality; to endure over time

[154] mighty or virtuous works, commanding influence; "of might" occurs in *As You Like It*, III v. 82.

[155] those who remain at court and fail to prove their valor in battle.

[156] cf. *Henry VI, Part 3* Act IV, scene 6—Henry: "Let me entreat, for I command no more."

[157] Mark Anderson, in his *"Shakespeare" by Another Name* blog (April 12, 2015), was kind enough to say of this chapter: "Here's why Waugaman's find matters: If it were indeed Oxford writing these words, it'd be one of the more 'Shakespearean' poems in his canon of early verse. For here is a poem that could be a kind of early draft of a speech from one of the many Anne Cecil-inspired heroines in the canon: Helena and Hermia come to mind in particular here. The former for her contending with a lover who has run off to Italy. The latter for a pathetic appeal she makes to her man citing the baby they have (she says) in common...If Waugaman's attribution is correct, it's Oxford in his full youthful voice -- bold, unabashed and arrogant. But then channeling that through the voice of a self-

effacing and modest gentlewoman who might be an understudy for a number of early Shakespearean heroines."

[158] Steven May, a leading anti-Oxfordian expert on de Vere's early signed poetry, agreed that the "poem's speaker seems to be in exactly the state of Anne De Vere during her husband's sojourn" in Italy (personal communication, July 27, 2010). However, May did not accept my attribution of the poem to Edward de Vere.

[159] I would ask the reader to give the poem a first reading now, before continuing to read my discussion of it.

[160] Rollins, Hyder E. (ed.), *Gorgious Gallery*. (Cambridge, Harvard University Press, 1926.)

[161] in her review of *Anna Komnene: The Life and Work of a Medieval Historian. London Review of Books*, 2 March 2017, p. 21.

[162] These verses use "fraught" meaning "to supply or furnish with" (OED 3.a.); the OED lists Munday's use as the second instance of this meaning, whereas the first is by de Vere's uncle Arthur Golding, in 1571.

[163] *Early English Books Online*

[164] Gerard Kilroy (personal communication, February 16, 2011) tentatively believes the following undated epigram by John Harington concerns these doubts as to the paternity of Anne's child: "While Caius doth remayne beyond the seas/ to follow there some great important sute,/ his land beares neither wheat, nor oats, nor peas,/ but yet his wife bare fayr and full grown frute./ Now what thinke you, doth cause his lands sterrillity,/ and his wives fruitfullnes and great fertillity,/ His Lands want occupiers to manure them,/ but she hath store [livestock used for breeding], and knowes how to procure [to obtain an illicit sexual partner] them." (text is from the manuscript copy of 400 epigrams prepared by Harington for Prince Henry in 1605 [Folger Shakespeare Library MS V.a.249].)

[165] "A Wanderlust Poem, Newly Attributed to Edward de Vere," *Shakespeare Matters* 7(1):21-23 (2007); the poem is reprinted in *Brief Chronicles* 2:264-265. Its title is *A young Gentleman willing to travell into forreygne partes, being intreated to staie in England: Wrote as followeth*. It was first published in the 1585 edition of *Paradise of Daintie Devises*.

[166] "*The Arte of English Poesie:* The Case for Edward de Vere's Authorship." *Brief Chronicles: The Interdisciplinary Journal of the Shakespeare Fellowship* 2:121-141 (2010).

[167] Whigham, Frank and Wayne A. Rebhorn (eds.), *The Art of English Poesie* (1589). (Ithaca, NY, Cornell University Press, 2007).

[168] See Anderson (2005), p. 189.

[169] I stumbled upon this poem while researching the astonishingly rich literary sources for "A Lover's Complaint." I found that the phrase "nature's outwards" in LC (line 80) echoed "nature outwardly" in "An other louing Letter," the second poem following YGW (it begins, "Because my hart is not mine owne, but resteth now with thee") . Both phrases allude to a pleasing external appearance.

[170] *Shakespeare by Another Name: The Life of Edward de Vere, Earl of Oxford, the Man who was Shakespeare.* (New York: Gotham Books, 2005.)

[171] An anonymous reviewer for *Brief Chronicles* amplifies these points with some intriguing additions. The reviewer writes that "Oxford's uncle Henry Howard (Surrey) did this, writing poems in the voice of a woman, possibly his own wife, fretting about her husband being at sea. Surrey seems to have gotten this from Chaucer -- and both are key influences on the younger de Vere as poet. The practice of adopting other voices (for Oxford, probably with such items as the Vavasour Echo poem and certain Queen Elizabeth productions that are questioned and whose deceptive origins are possibly illuminated in *Two Gentlemen of Verona* and *As You Like It* and elsewhere) can be seen as a middle step between lyric poetry and drama, between experimentation in adoption of other voices and the creation of whole characters out of text. The voice of this poem does sometimes sound like Helena from *All's Well that Ends Well* (with those Anne Cecil connections implicit)."

[172] I am grateful to an anonymous reviewer of the article on which this chapter is based for highlighting this point.

[173] This source of *The Tempest* is mentioned in Roger Stritmatter and Lynne Kositsky, "O Brave New World: *The Tempest* and Peter Martyr's *De Orbe Novo*," *Critical Survey* 21:2 (fall, 2009) 7-42; in fact, they note it was known to James Halliwell in the 19th century.

[174] unexpectedly

[175] The poem is not divided into stanzas in its original printing. For greater readability, I have taken the (considerable) liberty of dividing it into 24 four-line stanzas of rhymed couplet "fourteeners"—i.e., seven iambs per line. (Rollins calls the meter the "ballad stanza"

(xxiv). The final verse breaks two such lines into four lines of four, three, four, and three iambs. The poem is paired with the following "A letter sent from beyond the Seaes to his lover, perswading her to continew her loue towardes him."

176 consider, suppose; earliest instance of "imagine when" in EEBO

177 This is the unique use of this word in all 483 EEBO books published in 1578. De Vere also used "scrybled" in one of his letters. The word usually meant "to write in haste," often a self-deprecatory term for one's own letter, as in the present instance.

178 unplanned; irregular

179 lacking any cares

180 Note that, as in the Sonnets, this verb in ungrammatical. With the sort of syntactical pivot that characterizes many Sonnets, the implication might be "Suppose that the lines you are reading *came* to be so blurry because of my grief."

181 De Vere often used "w" for "u" in his letters. "Prowd" was the spelling used in only three other 1578 EEBO books, compared with 26 books that spelled the word "proud."

182 The earliest example of "proud disdain" in EEBO is Edward Hall's 1548 *The Union of the two Noble and Illustre Houses of Lancastre and Yorke*, an important source for Shakespeare.

183 The earliest use of "surpassing grief" in EEBO.

184 full of care

185 sealed note

186 cf. "tears distilled" from Sonnet 119.

187 proclaim

188 Hyder E. Rollins traces this "very common" allusion to a tiger as a trope for callousness back to Dido's reproach to Aeneas in Virgil's *Aeneid*, IV, after she discovers he plans to abandon her: "No goddess was your mother!/ No Dardanus sired [*auctor*: father; or author] your line, you traitor, liar, no,/ Mount Caucasus fathered you on its flinty rugged flanks/ and the tigers of Hyrcania gave you their dugs to suck!" (Robert Fagles, translator, 457-459).

189 Cf. 1534 "A prayer for the molifeing and suplyeng of our harde hertes..." with the words "*Molifie* and make softe our *harde hertes*, blessed father, which be indured and hardened with the cursed custome of synne and wretchednes" (emphasis added); from *A prymer in Englyshe for certeyn prayers and godly meditations*. (London: Johan Byddell, 1534). Echoing a prayer subtly enlists God

on the side of the Gentlewoman.

[190] Note the 18 words in the poem that begin with the prefix "re-," including especially "remember" (five times) and "return" (also five times).

[191] Deceitful, which might allude to de Vere's accusation that his wife's first child was fathered by another man.

[192] reform

[193] "loving mate" is found in Lewicke's 1562 translation of Boccaccio's *Titus and Gisippus*, and in Lyly's 1578 *Euphues*.

[194] encumbered by a sticky substance—i.e., her tears; the only prior instance in EEBO is in John Dee's 1577 *General and rare memorials*, in "beclogged with supersitition."

[195] "most unhappy state" used in Norton's 1565 *Gorboduc*, among other uses.

[196] The earliest example of "luckless star" in EEBO; there is a single earlier use of "lucky star."

[197] The earliest example of "frowning god" in EEBO.

[198] The second example of "hellish hag" in EEBO; the third is Robert Greene's 1584 *Gwyndonius the carde of fancie*.

[199] The only prior use of "furious fate" in EEBO was in Gascoigne's 1573 *Hundreth sundrie flowres*—in *Jocasta*, by Gascoigne and Kindlemarsh, first performed in 1566; its third use was in Shakespeare's *Henry V*.

[200] take after

[201] i.e., he is not your kinsman

[202] i.e., Aeneas

[203] "soyle" and "toyle" are also rhymed in "A young gentleman willing to travel" (YGM).

[204] faithful mate: earliest example in EEBO is Arthur Brooke's *Romeo and Juliet*; "feere" in the sense of "mate" occurs eight times in Golding's *Metamorphoses*, VII,84—this is much more often than its use in other early books listed in EEBO.

[205] attractive body

[206] "bygone." This is the earliest use of the word as an adjective in EEBO (it is much earlier than the only example of this usage given in the OED).

[207] This line illustrates a sort of "broken" or "dissected" alliteration that C.S. Lewis found in Shakespeare. Lewis gave an example from *Lucrece*: "To stamp the seal of time" (line 941); he noted that the

first two consonants of "stamp" are repeated in "seal" and "time," respectively. This line of the 1578 poem has "spent," followed by "sweet," and later "playes."

[208] slave

[209] excellent wenches

[210] Flirtatious or wanton

[211] recall

[212] only the second instance of "blame and hate" in EEBO.

[213] remember

[214] Note the two pairs of Shakespearean hendiadys in this line. "Heart and life" is used only four prior times in EEBO.

[215] prattling (also telling secrets)

[216] named above

[217] Only prior use of "wretched dame" was in Gascoigne's 1573 *Hundreth Sundrie Flowres*—it is used four times in his *Jocasta* there. *Flowres* includes an early use of "untwynd," also used in *2 Henry IV*; *Jocasta* likewise includes the earliest use in EEBO of "undisguised"—cf. de Vere's pattern of coining words beginning "un-" (as well as his use of both fictional and literary disguises). De Vere has been proposed as the actual author of Gascoigne's book.

[218] The only prior use noted in EEBO was in Gascoigne's *Flowres*, near the end of the book (where it occurs twice in three lines). "Thou hast thy will" occurs in Sonnet 135, as well as in *3 Henry VI*. Here, "will" suggests a pun, alluding not only to the husband's willfullness (i.e., "You're getting your *wish*"), but also his *lust* for the "Italian Dames."

[219] i.e., Jason

[220] to cease from action or speaking

[221] cf. the parallel allusion in YGM: "If *Jason* of that minde had binne... The golden fleece had binne to winne."

[222] If her husband abandons her as Jason did Medea, she will avenge herself by killling their child, as Medea did. However, this resolve softens after only one line.

[223] prevent ; among earlier uses was Gascoigne, ibid.

[224] to answer in a suitable way; EEBO's second example of "serve thy turn" comes from Matthew Parker's translation of the psalms— "The moone by night shall serve thy turne."

[225] i.e., he cannot accuse her of infidelity

[226] return

[227] This is the earliest example of "friendly gale" in EEBO; cf. the similar image of a "prosperous gale" in de Vere's April 27, 1603 letter to Robert Cecil about the personal impact of Queen Elizabeth's death.

[228] The third example of "happy port" in EEBO; the earliest is Arthur Brooke's *Romeo and Juliet*.

[229] This is the unique instance of the spelling "Scyrens" (for Sirens") in EEBO. And it was characteristic of de Vere to use "sc-" where his contemporaries used only "s-": he wrote "abscence" in one of his letters. Similarly, Hand D in a scene of the manuscript of *Sir Thomas More*, allegedly in the handwriting of "Shakespeare," includes the spelling "scilens" (for "silence").

[230] strategem

[231] put up with

[232] priestess

[233] the five short phrases in this line enact the speaker "ranging about."

[234] determined; also aimed

[235] turn

[236] dirtied

[237] The earliest example of "endless tears" in EEBO.

[238] The earliest example of "ugly dreams" in EEBO; several subsequent examples link them with disturbed sleep, as in this instance.

[239] devoid

[240] Here, I take "dispisde" as a misprint for a more apt, if newly coined word. "Piled" means "of a fabric, having a pile or nap." "Despiled" would also allude to "despoiled" (which can mean "disrobed"). This conjecture seems more consistent than does the word "despisde" with the other imagery in this stanza about the speaker's face, sleep, and food being spoiled.

[241] The earliest example of "tender sprig" in EEBO.

[242] The earliest example of "no certain port" in EEBO.

[243] The earliest example of "penetrate thy breast" in EEBO.

[244] cf. "win renowne" and "golden fleece to win" in YGM

[245] cf. "bin"/"win" rhyme in YGM. Rollins says of this line, "The wife means that a desire for fame or action is not what has taken her husband to Italy" (185).

[246] to wander about with no serious object

[247] The earliest example of "love to gad abroad" in EEBO; cf. "abroad to rome" and "I must abroad" in YGM

[248] "Foreign coasts" was first used in EEBO by Gascoigne in *Flowres*: "As one that held his native soyle in skorne,/ In foraine coastes to feede his fantasie." "Native soyle" also links Gascoigne's poem with YGM.

[249] comment

[250] Here is a variation on the pattern noted by C.S. Lewis— "freendly" is followed by "reason," then by "face"—the first two consonants of the first word once again appear later, but this time, in reverse order.

[251] i.e., God

[252] pain

[253] i.e., her heart

[254] The final stanza, like the couplet of several Shakespeare sonnets, is completely monosyllabic. It is also dense with internal rhymes (each iamb rhymes), could be arranged as two "fourteeners," the meter of the rest of the poem—
"By mee, to thee, not mine, but thine, since Love doth move the same,
Thy mate, though late, doth wright, her light, thou well, canst tell, her name."
The final stanza is reminiscent of the final stanza of an anonymous poem subscribed "My lucke is losse" (possibly one of de Vere's pseudonyms) in *Paradise of Daintie Devises*. The poem's first line is, "I sigh? Why so? For sorrowe of her smart." The final stanza shifts from iambic pentameter to three iambs per line, with the same rhyme in all nine lines. That final stanza begins with a paraphrase of the beginning of the final stanza of the 1578 poem: "What is, or may be mine,/ That is, and shall be thine."

[255] Originally published in *Shakespeare Matters* 7:6-11, 2008

[256] Toiling—pronounced as three syllables

[257] creature—animal or human

[258] erratic

[259] note the "wave" present in this word, anticipating "seas"

[260] this is the earliest use of "sweet repose" listed in Early English Books Online (EEBO). It was then used in the play *Arden of Haversham*, to which Shakespeare may have contributed (cf. *Shakespeare Quarterly*, 2006). It became a popular phrase in many

later works by other authors.

[261] out of one's house; outdoors [2 Henry IV—"your Lordship abroad"]; into foreign lands [Macbeth]

[262] i.e., when the snail is no longer governed by reason

[263] the misprint "Sayle" in the 1585 edition is corrected to "Snaile" in the 1596 edition

[264] art, expertness, sense of what is right

[265] guide, control; curb, restrain, check

[266] foolish

[267] mental faculties

[268] unoccupied time [Sonnet 39]; opportunity afforded by freedom from occupations [Much Ado]

[269] "work thy will"—to perform, carry out, execute [occurs elsewhere in 1596 edition, as well as in Munday's John a Kent— "Leave the God of Heaven to work his will"]

[270] "Dame reason" was referred to several times in Christine de Pisan's *The City of Ladies*

[271] slow

[272] bring about

[273] several people

[274] an archaic meaning, as an adjective, is "native born"

[275] Quintus Fabius Maximus, a 3d century B.C. Roman general of the second Punic war who was known for the success of his cautious military strategies; he tried to wear Hannibal down by avoiding pitched battles

[276] refers to a hawk descending swiftly on either its prey or to the lure

[277] a living bird such as a pigeon, used to entice a hawk into a net

[278] hasty, impetuous, rash

[279] clever [used in that sense by Holinshed]

[280] to enfold, clothe; to coil, to wrap as in a garment. Changed to "lay" in 1596 edition

[281] unless

[282] ill-will, malice [Merchant of Venice]; envy in its current meaning [Julius Caesar]; plural—jealousies, rivalries. The word was changed to "envious" in all editions subsequent to 1585.

[283] nets

[284] in spite of; spelled "maugur" in 1596 edition

[285] something imaginary [Romeo—"Love… made with the fume of

sighs"]; something which clouds the reason [*The Tempest*—"the ignorant fumes"]

[286] Rollins (1927) glosses this line as meaning "Except for the fretting of those who envy you, there are few who shall harm you, no matter how much the envious may fume" (p. 269).

[287] caused (literally, "worked")

[288] follows

[289] infirm; pronounced as two syllables. Spelled "crazed" in 1596 edition

[290] Rollins notes that "crased sore was a favorite expression of the Elizabethans; *sore* is an adverb, and the phrase means those who are very infirm or sorely injured" (p. 269). However, I found no other examples in EEBO.

[291] "virtues in degree" alludes to traditional medieval beliefs in the hierarchy of seven virtues—three were theological (faith, hope, and charity, all three resulting from grace, and all three necessary for salvation) and four were moral (prudence, justice, temperance, and fortitude). The phrase also alludes to Aquinas's influential synthesis of virtues, incorporating Aristotle's "habitus," which refers to man's capacity to act well or badly

[292] "in spight of spight" was a phrase used in Shakespeare's *King John*, and in Philip Sidney's *His Astrophel and Stella*. It was also used by George Pettie in his 1581 translation of Stefano Girazzo's *Civile Conversation*—"in spight of spight shee [Queen Elizabeth[will triumph over all yll tongues."

[293] Rollins believes "I weare thee still" means "as my device (as in a shield or coat of arms)" (p. 269)

[294] unless otherwise specified, I am referring to the Geneva Bible owned by de Vere

[295] the numbers of some of the sonnets are closely linked with their content. The number of this sonnet, 121, lists the number of letters in the words "I am I." In addition, the two Arabic numbers 1 resemble the word "I." cf. also "I am I" in Richard III, V, iii

[296] in the Sternhold Metrical Psalms bound at the end of de Vere's Geneva Bible, Psalm 58:8 is translated as "As snailes do wast within the shel,/ And unto slime do run:/ As one before his tyme that fel,/ And never saw the sunne." De Vere annotated his metrical psalms far more than he did the version of the psalms bound in his Old Testament.

[297] Psalms 58:3 referred to the womb: "The wicked are strangers from the wombe: even from the belly have they erred, and speak lies." The seventh verse anticipates some of the imagery of the eighth: "Let them [the wicked] melt like the waters, let them passe away: when he shooteth his arrowes, let them be as broken."

[298] yes, that was 13 iambs, like each couplet in our poem

[299] dangerous fluid accumulation in the fetus

[300] cf. my article on that poem in *Shakespeare Matters* (2007)

[301] these words are also rhymed in "A young Gentleman will to travell into forreygne partes," which I have previously attributed to de Vere (Waugaman, 2007)

[302] From John Davies (ed.), *Epigrammes and Elegies by I.D. and C.M.*, Middleborugh [sic], 1599.

[303] This section was first published in *Shakespeare Matters* 11(3):6, 2012.

[304] The first instance of this hendiadys in EEBO.

[305] An abbreviated version of this section was presented at Frank Whigham and Wayne A. Rebhorn's Seminar on *The Arte of English Poesie* at the Annual Meeting of the Shakespeare Association of America, April 9, 2009. I am grateful to Steven May for his helpful comments on my paper. This chapter originally appeared in *Brief Chronicles* 2:121-141, 2010.

[306] Whigham and Rebhorn placed special emphasis on the cart and court trope in the *Arte*. It is therefore noteworthy that the poem "In praise of a contented mind" that Steven May believes may be written by de Vere contains the line "The Court ne cart I like ne loath." The poem was first published in 1588, just a year before the *Arte*.

[307] De Vere's older half-sister Katherine married a relative of George Puttenham (his wife's stepson). See Willis (2003, p. 258).

[308] Yes, I am speculating. So do Schoenbaum, Greenblatt, and others. Not surprisingly, I find my speculations more plausible than theirs.

[309] Internal evidence suggests the *Arte* was in fact written around 1586.

[310] The annual budget of the Office of Revels was reduced by roughly 1,000 pounds per year around the same time (Streitberger, 2008, 200).

[311] In Book 1, chapter 8. Further examples are on 148f, 196f, 362,

etc. (all page references are to Whigham and Rebhorn's edition). This practice is burlesqued in *The Tempest* by Stephano, when he promises that "Wit shall not go unrewarded while I am king of this country" (IV,1,241).

[312] I plan to present these discoveries in a forthcoming book. An excellent digitized version of de Vere's Bible is now available on-line, on the Folger Shakespeare Library's website. The manicules and other annotations are clearly visible.

[313] Although Roger Stritmatter (2001) did not find these psalm echoes in Shakespeare's work, he did note the psalm manicules, and it was his ground-breaking work that led me to research de Vere's Bible.

[314] cf. the *Arte*'s "the new *devices* are ever *dainty*" (p. 244).

[315] Waugaman, 2007 and 2008.

[316] The early owner of one first edition especially ridiculed the geometric poetic forms, writing in his copy [Folger STC 20519 (5)], "The puerile absurdity of mechanical versifying is fully displayed by Puttenham's table of geometrical figures... [T]he author must have been seized by a poetic cramp." Alastair Fowler, by contrast, argued that "These sections, often brushed aside as frivolous curiosities, should in some instances be seen as serious though fumbling attempts at a theory of numerical composition" (11). Fowler's and Blank's discussions of the role of number and measurement in the *Arte* and in Shakespeare's works are consistent with the great interest de Vere showed in Biblical passages dealing with numbers. The first Biblical passage that De Vere annotated in his Geneva Bible was Genesis 18: 26-- "And the Lord answered, If I finde in Sodom fifty righteous within the citie, then will I spare all the place for their sakes." Waugaman ("Shakespeare's Sonnet 6 and the First Marked Passage in de Vere's Bible," *Shakespeare Matters* [in press-b]) argues that this verse and its context are an important source for Sonnet 6. I Samuel, which de Vere annotated most densely, has 18 different numbers among its marked verses. II Samuel has 14 numbers among *its* marked verses. De Vere underlined only the phrase with numbers in I Kings 8: 63-- "And Solomon offred a sacrifice of peace offrings which he offred unto the Lord, to wit, *two and twentie thousand beeves, and a hundreth and twentie thousand shepe*: so the King and all the children of Israel dedicated the house of the Lord." He also wrote in the margin next to this verse, "Oxen

240

22000; shepe 1220000 [sic]."

[317] In *Cymbeline*, Jachimo uses as evidence that he has been intimate with Imogen his description that "under her breast... lies a mole" (V.ii.134-135). [I am grateful to an anonymous reviewer for bringing this parallel to my attention.]

[318] See my review of North's book in *Shakespeare Matters*, 8(3):20, 25, 26, 2009.

[319] Much of the *Arte* seems modeled on Castiglione's *The Book of the Courtier,* for which de Vere wrote a prefatory letter. Further, the *Arte* competes with *The Defense of Poetry* by Philip Sidney, one of de Vere's arch-rivals (d. 1586).

[320] In the eight unnumbered pages that intriguingly survive only in Ben Jonson's copy, perhaps because they include this anagram that called the Queen "aged." She was notoriously sensitive about her age. The *Arte*'s hostility toward the Queen is consistent with her exiling de Vere from court for two years in 1581. Ben Jonson's copy, by the way, had marginal manicules, according to Whigham and Rebhorn. Were they drawn by de Vere?

[321] Chicago, University of Chicago Press, 2014.

[322] She did confirm that she doubts Puttenham was the author—"let the *Arte* work its magic anonymously" (personal communication, April 8, 2009).

[323] This sentence in Chap. 31, Book 1, ends with "that noble gentleman *Edward* Earle of Oxford." Edward Arber's 1906 reprint retained that full stop, whereas Whighman and Reborn apparently read the period as a typo and replaced it with a comma. However, the subsequent sentence is ungrammatical either way. I would argue that their comma inadvertently deprives de Vere of his rightful prominence in this section. Any injustice the comma does to de Vere, however, pales in comparison with Alan Nelson"s prejudicial ODNB revision of the far more objective 1899 DNB biography of de Vere.

[324] Cf. his quoting the maxim "Qui nescit dissimulare nescit regnare" ["Who cannot dissemble, cannot rule"] (271).

[325] The internet, of course, is reviving authorial anonymity.

[326] Cf. John Mullan (2007).

[327] The *Arte*'s author mentions his comedy *Ginecocratia* (218) and his interlude *Lusty London* (256).

[328] *Romeo and Juliet* 2.2.76.

329 *Macbeth* 3.4.30.
330 *Macbeth* 3.4.95.
331 *Merchant of Venice* 3.4.76.
332 *Tempest* 2.1.308.
333 *Merchant of Venice* 1.2.61.
334 *Merchant of Venice* 3.2.286.
335 *Anthony and Cleopatra* 1.5.70.
336 *Romeo and Juliet* 4.2.2.
337 *Richard III* 4.2.41.
338 *Merry Wives of Windsor* 1.1.2-3.
339 *Merry Wives of Windsor* 2.2.68.
340 *Julius Caesar* 1.3.17.
341 *Richard II* 2.2.14.
342 *Titus Andronicus* 5.1.22.
343 *Winter's Tale* 4.3.42.
344 *Merry Wives of Windsor* 5.5.77.
345 *Timon of Athens* 1.1.267.
346 *Titus Andronicus* 5.1.78.
347 *3 Henry VI* 3.2.168.
348 Rudolph Gotfried (ed.), John Harington's *Orlando Furioso*. Bloomington: University of Indiana Press, 1963, xix.
349 Peter R. Moore, 'The Stella Coverup." *Shakespeare Oxford Society Newsletter* 29:12-17, 1993.
350 Although folklorists are now sceptical of this explanation, their attempts to dismiss this theory as a false myth have generated lively and contentious debates on the discussion page of the relevant Wikipedia article. We should not forget that anthropologists were similarly dismissive of Putarch's description of the intoxicating gasses that caused trances for the priestesses of Apollo at Delphi, until John Hale's recent research completely vindicated Plutarch.
351 This section was first published in *Shakespeare Matters* 11(3):6, 2012

352 Norman Egbert McClure (ed.), *The Letters and Epigrams of Sir John Harington.* Philadelphia: University of Pennsylvania Press, 1930, p. 51.
353 Katherine Duncan-Jones, a highly respected Stratfordian, hints ever so subtly in her 2007 *Shakespeare's Poems* (London: Arden, 2007) that she realizes Ignoto and Shake-speare may be the same

poet—she reproduces in an appendix p. 169 of the 1602 first edition, showing a facsimile of "The first" and "The burning" so that readers can see for themselves that "Let the bird of loudest lay" seems to be a continuation of those poems. Even the "printers' flowers," used rarely in this volume, occur below the name "Ignoto," and later below the name "William Shake-speare." She also observes that "The burning" uses "quasi-theatrical language" (p. 112).

[354] A 1602 Ignoto poem in Francis Davison's anthology *A Poetical Rapsodie* is titled, "An Invective Against Women." It contains the phrase, "they will beguile ye." The only previous use of that phrase in EEBO is found in a 1530 edition of Sir John Oldcastle's 1413 "Endenture" (edited by William Thorpe in *The examinacion of the honorable knight syr Jhon Oldcastell*, Antwerp: J. van Hoochstraten) which records his trial for heresy. One is tempted to conclude that de Vere read that book, and picked up that phrase, while researching the man who was transformed into Falstaff. (I am grateful to Robert Detobel for bringing Davison's anthology to my attention.)

[355] William Scott, *The Model of Poesy*, Gavin Alexander (ed.), Cambridge, Cambridge University Press,1599/2014.

[356] originally published in *Brief Chronicles* 2:260-266, 2010.

[357] Gerard Kilroy (ed.), *Epigrams of Sir John Harington*, Burlington, VT: Ashgate, 2009. Kilroy mentions de Vere as the only possible figure behind "Caius" (p. 338).

"Caius" appears in epigrams I.54; II.14, 19, 34, 55, 58; and IV.69.

[358] I.54. II.19 calls de Vere a "wittoll," or a contented cuckold.

[359] IV.16. Kilroy notes that Sir Henry Lee took Vavasour "as his mistress sometime around 1590, and openly proclaimed her as such at tournaments, with "A.V. Lelia" engraved on his armour." This date of 1590 raises the possibility that Vavasour may be the unfaithful Dark Lady of the Sonnets.

[360] Samuel Fallon and David Scott Kastan reported that, in 2011, the Beinecke Library at Yale acquired fragments of lost books that include three of the Partheniades poems, poems that otherwise survived only in manuscript form in the British Library. That manuscript states that "the Author intended not to have his name knowne." They acknowledge that there is still doubt as to the authorship of these poems, and of the *Arte* ("scholars generally agree" it was Puttenham); study of the newly studied fragments "does not settle the issue of authorship" (*TLS*, February 5, 2016, p.

14).

[361] North made this clear in a personal communication on April 9, 2009.

[362] The poem and my article on it are reprinted elsewhere in this book.

[363] a rhetorical figure in which a word is recalled, then replaced with a more correct one.

[364] The first use of this word recorded by EEBO; a rhetorical term for wordplay, punning.

[365] indirect modes of speech

[366] my subtitle is a rhetorical question, of course.

Made in the USA
Monee, IL
25 January 2022

89844846R00143